SCHOLASTIC

YEAR 1 PHOTOCOPIABLES

All you need to teach 11 curriculum subjects!

- Levelled and linked to the curriculum
- Stand-alone photocopiable activities
- Ideal for mixed-age classes

AGES 5-6

Paul Noble and Jean Noble

AUTHORS
Paul Noble and Jean Noble

DEVELOPMENT EDITOR
Kate Pedlar

PROJECT EDITOR
Fabia Lewis

DESIGNERS
Q2a Media

COVER DESIGN
Anna Oliwa

ILLUSTRATOR
Gaynor Berry

Mixed Sources
Product group from well-managed forests and other controlled sources
www.fsc.org Cert no. TT-COC-002769
© 1996 Forest Stewardship Council

Published by Scholastic Ltd
Book End
Range Road
Witney
Oxfordshire
OX29 0YD
www.scholastic.co.uk
Designed using Adobe InDesign
Printed by Bell & Bain Ltd, Glasgow

2 3 4 5 6 7 8 9 9 0 1 2 3 4 5 6 7

British Library Cataloguing-in-Publication Data
A catalogue record for this book is available from the British Library.

ISBN 978-1407-10093-7

Photocopiable pages first published in *Year Group Photocopiables Year 1* (first published 2002).

CONTENTS

CONTENTS

INTRODUCTION

This is a straightforward compilation of stand-alone photocopiable activities for children in Year 1.

Ranging across the curriculum as they do, the activities within this book provide material for the National Curriculum subjects (except PE) plus Religious Education, PSHE and Citizenship. Although understandably not comprehensive in its National Curriculum coverage, this volume brings together a selection of previously published Scholastic photocopiables that have all been successfully tried and tested. You can use them with confidence and No Fuss.

At the heart of the book are the activity sheets presented with a concise and factual **curriculum grid**, which, in note form, cross-references the content of the sheets to the National Curriculum, the Primary Framework, QCA schemes of work and where appropriate, to the Curriculum for Excellence (Scotland). Objectives for each activity sheet are stated and brief guidance notes are given to its use.

Within the curriculum grid, links are made to National Curriculum Attainment Targets and attainment levels as well as to the non-statutory Attainment Targets for RE and the non-statutory guidelines at Key Stage 1 for PSHE and Citizenship.

Before you use any worksheet it is recommended that you refer to the curriculum grid so that you are clear about the objectives and are aware of any special demands made by the activity.

In Year 1, children are usually well-socialised into the norms of behaviour in a school community, and face a year unsullied by standard prescribed tests. It is a particularly enjoyable year to teach, as there is an eagerness to learn coupled, very often, with a cheerful bright-eyed, bushy-tailed innocence that helps to offset the sweat and toil involved. The *No Fuss* books are intended to ease some of this toil and mop up some of the sweat. You will find this book particularly helpful when you are limited by time or have to meet the needs of voracious learners. Supply teachers and others 'caught on the hop' will also be able to rely on this material to help them to cope with demanding days.

You will hardly need reminding that although these worksheets will support your teaching, they cannot do it for you. A whole school full of over-heated photocopiers will not make children learn; it is for you to capture their interest and to provide the intellectual stimulus and practical experience that needs to accompany learning.

Page	Activity	Objectives	Teachers' notes	NC, QCA & Primary Framework	Curriculum for Excellence (Scotland)	AT links and levels
15	Rhyme and count	To learn different ways to spell phonemes by practising the ability to rhyme.	The cutting, sticking and ordering must follow lots of oral work on the rhyme. The oral work is the key to this exercise.	Literacy Strand 2 – Listening and responding; Strand 5 – Word recognition	LIT 002A/L/W – Enjoyment and choice (reading) LIT 010N/X – Tools for reading	AT2 Level 1 AT3 Level 1
16	Nobody spoke	To practise the ability to rhyme and to develop rhyming strings.	Good listening is necessary to appreciate rhyme. Practise making up variations such as 'Wendy and Bill were silent and still'.	Literacy Strand 2 – Listening and responding; Strand 5 – Word recognition	LIT 002A/L/W – Enjoyment and choice (reading) LIT 010N/X – Tools for reading	AT2 Level 1 AT3 Level 1
17	Rhyme lines	To sort CVC words into rhyming sets.	Read the words aloud first. Get the children to recite the rhyming strings to an adult afterwards.	Literacy Strand 2 – Listening and responding; Strand 5 – Word recognition	LIT 002A/L/W – Enjoyment and choice (reading) LIT 010N/X – Tools for reading	AT2 Level 1 AT3 Level 1
18	Lewis' ladder game	To begin to hear initial and final phonemes in CVC words and to be able to sound out and blend all three phonemes.	Lewis Carroll is credited with inventing this game, hence the name. Ensure you direct the children to the picture clues.	Literacy Strand 2 – Listening and responding; Strand 5 – Word recognition	LIT 002A/L/W – Enjoyment and choice (reading) LIT 010N/X – Tools for reading	AT2 Level 1 AT3 Level 1
19	Word factory	To learn to read and spell words ending in double consonants -ff, -ll and -ss.	Confirm that the double consonants are known. Encourage children to experiment.	Literacy Strand 2 – Listening and responding; Strand 5 – Word recognition; Strand 6 – Word structure and spelling	LIT 010N/X – Tools for reading LIT 120X – Tools for writing	AT2 Level 1 AT3 Level 1
20	Spelling bee	To learn to read and spell words ending in -ck and -ng.	The bee goes from a petal to the centre of the flower making a word as it does so. Talk about bees.	Literacy Strand 2 – Listening and responding; Strand 5 – Word recognition; Strand 6 – Word structure and spelling	LIT 010N/X – Tools for reading LIT 120X – Tools for writing	AT2 Level 1 AT3 Level 1
21	Word slide	To learn to read and spell words that begin with different consonant clusters.	Mount the sheet onto card for ease of use. Explain that not all combinations are valid words.	Literacy Strand 2 – Listening and responding; Strand 5 – Word recognition; Strand 6 – Word structure and spelling	LIT 010N/X – Tools for reading LIT 120X – Tools for writing	AT2 Level 1 AT3 Level 1
22	Beginnings	To learn to read and spell words that begin with the consonant clusters fl-, fr-, sn- and spr-.	Sound out the consonant clusters to ensure that they are known before proceeding.	Literacy Strand 2 – Listening and responding; Strand 5 – Word recognition; Strand 6 – Word structure and spelling	LIT 010N/X – Tools for reading LIT 120X – Tools for writing	AT2 Level 1 AT3 Level 1
23	Finish the job (1)	To learn to read and spell words that end with the consonant clusters -ld, -nd, -lk and -nk.	Another variation of the same idea as before. The less confident may need help to identify the pictures.	Literacy Strand 2 – Listening and responding; Strand 5 – Word recognition; Strand 6 – Word structure and spelling	LIT 010N/X – Tools for reading LIT 120X – Tools for writing	AT2 Level 1 AT3 Level 1
24	Finish the job (2)	To learn to read and spell words that end with the consonant clusters -st, -nch, -mp and -sk.	This is a variation on the previous sheet and can be tackled in a similar way.	Literacy Strand 2 – Listening and responding; Strand 5 – Word recognition; Strand 6 – Word structure and spelling	LIT 010N/X – Tools for reading LIT 120X – Tools for writing	AT2 Level 1 AT3 Level 1
25	Say and spell: 'ea' in seat	To begin to recognise different spelling patterns for the phoneme *ea*.	Make sure that children recognise and can sound out the long vowel sound *ea*. Encourage them to say the word before writing it down.	Literacy Strand 2 – Listening and responding; Strand 5 – Word recognition; Strand 6 – Word structure and spelling	LIT 010N/X – Tools for reading LIT 120X – Tools for writing	AT2 Level 1 AT3 Level 1
26	Say and spell: 'ee' in weep	To begin to recognise spelling patterns for the phoneme *ee*.	Follow the same procedure as above.	Literacy Strand 2 – Listening and responding; Strand 5 – Word recognition; Strand 6 – Word structure and spelling	LIT 010N/X – Tools for reading LIT 120X – Tools for writing	AT2 Level 1 AT3 Level 1
27	Say and spell: 'ai' in paid	To begin to recognise spelling patterns for the phoneme *ai*.	Follow the same procedure as before.	Literacy Strand 2 – Listening and responding; Strand 5 – Word recognition; Strand 6 – Word structure and spelling	LIT 010N/X – Tools for reading LIT 120X – Tools for writing	AT2 Level 1 AT3 Level 1
28	Say and spell: 'igh' in light	To begin to recognise spelling patterns for the phoneme *igh*.	Make sure that the children recognise and can sound out the long vowel phoneme *igh*. Speak then write.	Literacy Strand 2 – Listening and responding; Strand 5 – Word recognition; Strand 6 – Word structure and spelling	LIT 010N/X – Tools for reading LIT 120X – Tools for writing	AT2 Level 1 AT3 Level 1

Page	Activity	Objectives	Teachers' notes	NC, QCA & Primary Framework	Curriculum for Excellence (Scotland)	AT links and levels
29	Say and spell: 'oa' in boat	To begin to recognise spelling patterns for the phoneme *oa*.	Make sure that children can recognise and sound out the long vowel phoneme *oa*. Speak before writing down.	Literacy Strand 2 – Listening and responding; Strand 5 – Word recognition; Strand 6 – Word structure and spelling	LIT 010N/X – Tools for reading LIT 120X – Tools for writing	AT2 Level 1 AT3 Level 1
30	Say and spell: 'oo' in hoot	To begin to recognise different spelling patterns for the phoneme *oo* (as in boot).	Make sure that children can recognise and sound out the long vowel phoneme *oo*. Speak before writing down.	Literacy Strand 2 – Listening and responding; Strand 5 – Word recognition; Strand 6 – Word structure and spelling	LIT 010N/X – Tools for reading LIT 120X – Tools for writing	AT2 Level 1 AT3 Level 1
31	Dream sentences	To recognise when a sentence does not make sense.	Ask the children to identify who is dreaming in proper sentences. Reading/speaking before colouring is the key.	Literacy Strand 2 – Listening and responding; Strand 11 – Sentence structure and punctuation	LIT 006G/T – Understanding, analysing and evaluating (reading) LIT 121Y – Tools for writing	AT1 Level 1 AT2 Level 1 AT3 Level 1
32	Build brick sentences	To know how to use capital letters and full stops in simple sentences. To be able to reorder the words in a sentence so that it makes sense.	This is not as easy as it might seem. There are pitfalls. Demonstrate by completing an example and challenge the children to make five or six more. More can be made by using a brick more than once but the sheet will then become complicated and possibly messy.	Literacy Strand 2 – Listening and responding; Strand 11 – Sentence structure and punctuation	LIT 006G/T – Understanding, analysing and evaluating (reading) LIT 121Y – Tools for writing	AT2 Level 1 AT3 Level 1
33	Say and write: same sounds	To learn spelling patterns for the long vowel phonemes *a-e, i-e, o-e and u-e*.	Explain the examples in the left-hand column. The children complete the rest by imitation and deduction.	Literacy Strand 2 – Listening and responding; Strand 5 – Word recognition; Strand 6 – Word structure and spelling	LIT 010N/X – Tools for reading LIT 120X – Tools for writing	AT2 Level 1
34	Capital beginnings	To learn to use capital letters for the beginning of a sentence.	Complete some examples for the children first.	Literacy Strand 2 – Listening and responding; Strand 5 – Word recognition; Strand 11 – Sentence structure and punctuation	LIT 010N/X – Tools for reading LIT 121Y – Tools for writing	AT2 Level 1 AT3 Level 1/2
35	Missing titles	To be able to read and write book titles using capital letters correctly.	The sheet should only be used following an exploration of book titles, where they are written, how they are written and so on. Show (read and enjoy!) an example, such as *Harry's Mad*.	Literacy Strand 2 – Listening and responding; Strand 11 – Sentence structure and punctuation	LIT 010N/X – Tools for reading LIT 121Y – Tools for writing	AT2 Level 1 AT3 Level 1/2
36	Hands up!	To learn to add question marks to questions.	Explain what a question is – questions demand answers – and that they require the use of question marks when written down.	Literacy Strand 2 – Listening and responding; Strand 11 – Sentence structure and punctuation	LIT 010N/X – Tools for reading LIT 121Y – Tools for writing	AT2 Level 1 AT3 Level 1/2
37	Story sense	To recognise the beginning, middle and ending of a story and to use this knowledge to retell a story in the correct order.	Cut up the sheet before handing it out. This makes a good small-group activity.	Literacy Strand 2 – Listening and responding; Strand 7 – Understanding and interpreting texts; Strand 10 – Text structure and organisation	LIT 006GT – Understanding, analysing and evaluating (reading)	AT2 Level 1/2
38	Rick Wrong and Rose Right	To recognise when a sentence does not make sense. To use contextual and other clues to order sentences correctly.	The words are muddled but no additional words are needed for it to make sense. Emphasise that Rick is always wrong and Rose is always right.	Literacy Strand 2 – Listening and responding; Strand 7 – Understanding and interpreting texts; Strand 11 – Sentence structure and punctuation	LIT 006GT – Understanding, analysing and evaluating (reading)	AT2 Level 1/2 AT3 Level 1
39	Football numbers	To be able to count in order in ones and twos.	A straightforward counting exercise.	Maths Strand – Counting and understanding number	MNU 001B – Number processes	AT2 Level 1
40	Jumping in tens	To improve counting backwards and forwards in tens.	Familiarity with the jumping strategy helps here. They should count the size of the jumps first.	Maths Strands – Using and applying mathematics; Knowing and using number facts	MNU 001B – Number processes MNU 002C – Addition, subtraction, multiplication and division	AT2 Level 1/2
41	Odds and evens	To count in twos and to begin to recognise odd and even numbers.	Get children to count out loud rhythmically. Count in twos from any number below 20.	Maths Strands – Counting and understanding number; Knowing and using number facts	MNU 001B – Number processes MNU 002C – Addition, subtraction, multiplication and division	AT2 Level 2

Page	Activity	Objectives	Teachers' notes	NC, QCA & Primary Framework	Curriculum for Excellence (Scotland)	AT links and levels
42	Missing numbers	To count forwards and backwards in steps of different sizes.	Draw children's attention to the mini number line at the side of the page.	Maths Strands – Using and applying mathematics; Counting and understanding number; Knowing and using number facts	MNU 001B – Number processes MNU 002C – Addition, subtraction, multiplication and division	AT2 Level 1/2
43	Writing numbers	To read and write numbers in figures and words.	Go through the completed example at the top. Note that there are more words at the bottom of the sheet than are needed.	Maths Strand – Counting and understanding number	MNU 001B – Number processes MNU 002C – Addition, subtraction, multiplication and division	AT2 Level 1
44	Tens and ones	To be able to partition a number into tens and ones.	Ideally a real abacus should be used alongside this sheet.	Maths Strand – Counting and understanding number	MNU 102B – Number processes	AT2 Level 2
45	More tens and ones	To be able to partition a number into tens and ones.	Support those who need it by providing some counting apparatus.	Maths Strand – Counting and understanding number	MNU 102B – Number processes	AT2 Level 2
46	Number splits	To be able to partition a number into tens and ones and into multiples of tens and ones.	Explaining the joke usually kills it but it will probably help children to complete the exercise if you do.	Maths Strand – Calculating	MNU 102B – Number processes	AT2 Level 2
47	In the queue	To learn the vocabulary of ordering numbers.	Only use this sheet when it has been preceded by oral work in the classroom.	Maths Strand – Counting and understanding number	MNU 102B – Number processes	AT2 Level 1
48	More than…	To be able to identify the number that is more than any given number up to 30.	Oral responses to the questions are more important than written responses so work with the class first.	Maths Strands – Using and applying mathematics; Counting and understanding number; Knowing and using number facts	MNU 001B – Number processes MNU 002C – Addition, subtraction, multiplication and division	AT2 Level 1/2
49	Less than…	To be able to identify the number that is one less than any given number up to 30.	Discuss the talking scarecrow with the class. Oral responses again take precedence over the written.	Maths Strands – Using and applying mathematics; Counting and understanding number; Knowing and using number facts	MNU 001B – Number processes MNU 002C – Addition, subtraction, multiplication and division	AT2 Level 1/2
50	Five faces	To learn addition facts for pairs of numbers that make 5.	Sub-dividing the set of 5 by colouring may need a little explanation. Stick to the same two colours throughout for clarity.	Maths Strands – Knowing and using number facts; Calculating	MNU 002C – Addition, subtraction, multiplication and division	AT2 Level 1
51	Six sailors	To learn addition facts for pairs of numbers that make 6.	The sailors are a counting aid that will not be needed by all children.	Maths Strands – Knowing and using number facts; Calculating	MNU 002C – Addition, subtraction, multiplication and division	AT2 Level 1
52	Ten tumblers	To be able to recall all pairs of numbers that total 10.	The gymnasts are just a more challenging version of the sailors in the previous sheet.	Maths Strands – Knowing and using number facts; Calculating	MNU 002C – Addition, subtraction, multiplication and division MTH 118R – Expressions and equations	AT2 Level 1/2
53	Sorting sheep	To count and order sets of familiar numbers.	Explain the exercise: the sheep should be counted first. Connecting the numbers smallest to largest can be made more interesting by asking children to go from field to field using the gates.	Maths Strands – Using and applying mathematics; Counting and understanding number	MNU 011W – Data and analysis MNU 001B – Number processes	AT2 Level 1/2
54	Three jumps to 6	To understand addition by using a number line.	Talk through the completed example so that the process is fully understood.	Maths Strands – Using and applying mathematics; Calculating	MNU 002C – Addition, subtraction, multiplication and division	AT2 Level 1
55	Three jumps to 10	To understand addition by using a number line.	This is an extension of the idea in the previous sheet.	Maths Strands – Using and applying mathematics; Calculating	MNU 002C – Addition, subtraction, multiplication and division	AT2 Level 1
56	Blank arithmetic	To add two numbers together using a number line as an aid.	Children need to be familiar with using number lines for counting on and understand what the blanks stand for.	Maths Strand – Calculating	MNU 002C – Addition, subtraction, multiplication and division MTH 118R Expressions and equations	AT2 Level 1/2

Page	Activity	Objectives	Teachers' notes	NC, QCA & Primary Framework	Curriculum for Excellence (Scotland)	AT links and levels
57	More blank arithmetic	To calculate the value of unknown numbers to complete number sentences.	In any number sentence the different shaped blanks do not stand for the same number. This is a tricky concept: the beginning of algebra.	Maths Strand – Calculating	MNU 002C – Addition, subtraction, multiplication and division MTH 118R – Expressions and equations	AT2 Level 2
58	Spending money	To solve money problems by adding and counting.	Similar problems can be practised orally and coins can be used to support the tasks on the sheet.	Maths Strand – Using and applying mathematics	MNU 004K; MNU 107K – Money	AT2 Level 1/2
59	Find the difference	To begin to use the vocabulary involved in subtracting, such as 'difference'.	If the children find the idea of difference difficult to grasp, use objects or counters to give the 'difference' a more concrete existence.	Maths Strands – Using and applying mathematics; Calculating	MNU 002C – Addition, subtraction, multiplication and division	AT2 Level 1
60	Guess Nelly's numbers	To begin to use the vocabulary involved in subtracting, such as 'take away' and 'subtract'.	Demonstrate the process of complementary addition (adding back what was taken away gets you back to where you started).	Maths Strands – Using and applying mathematics; Knowing and using number facts; Calculating	MNU 002C – Addition, subtraction, multiplication and division	AT2 Level 1
61	Seeing double	To be able to derive and recall doubles of numbers up to 6.	Go through the completed example. Use the term 'double' and challenge the children to remember the answers.	Maths Strands – Using and applying mathematics; Knowing and using number facts	MNU 002C – Addition, subtraction, multiplication and division MTH 118R – Expressions and equations	AT2 Level 1/2
62	Time passing	To use language, and solve simple problems, related to time.	You may well have to vary your approach with this sheet depending on where your children are starting from. Some children will manage unaided; others will manage as part of an oral exercise.	Maths Strand – Measuring	MNU 005L – Time	AT1 Level 1 AT2 Level 1/2
63	Sorting shapes	To describe features of 2D shapes.	Lots of oral and practical work should precede this sheet as children must understand the terms used.	Maths Strands – Using and applying mathematics; Understanding shape	MTH 008S – Properties of 2D shapes	AT3 Level 1/2
64	Where am I?	To use everyday words to describe position.	Oral work is needed to give this sheet value so an adult needs to be involved.	Maths Strand – Using and applying mathematics	MTH 009T/U – Angle, symmetry and transformation	AT3 Level 1
65	Am I an animal?	To understand that the term 'animal' includes humans.	Children will need to place the objects and animals into the correct set by drawing an arrow or cutting and sticking.	Science NC: Sc2 Life processes QCA: Unit 1A Ourselves	SCN 002B; SCN 102B – Biodiversity	AT1 Level 1 AT2 Level 1
66	Adults and young	To match adults and young of the same animals and to understand that animals grow and change over time.	You need to explain that adult animals no longer grow. Ask what the animals used to be like before they grew into adults.	Science NC: Sc2 Humans and other animals QCA: Unit 1A Ourselves	SCN 002B – Biodiversity	AT1 Level 1 AT2 Level 1/2
67	Alive and not alive	To distinguish between animals and inanimate objects.	Explain clearly the main differences between living and non-living things using the terms 'feed', 'move' and 'grow'.	Science NC: Sc2 Life processes QCA: Unit 1A Ourselves	SCN 102B – Biodiversity	AT1 Level 1/2 AT2 Level 1
68	Growing food	To understand that some plants provide food for humans.	Make sure that children understand that some plants are poisonous.	Science NC: Sc2 Humans and other animals; Sc2 Green plants QCA: Unit 1B Growing plants	SCN 002B – Biodiversity SCN 005H – Energy in food	AT1 Level 1/2 AT2 Level 1/2
69	Material mad	To understand that objects are made from materials and that different materials have different uses.	All the clothes are made from materials but not necessarily the best ones for the job. Create a 'materials' wordbank for the class to use.	Science NC: Sc3 Grouping materials QCA: Unit 1C Sorting and using materials	SCN 013X – Properties and uses	AT1 Level 1 AT3 Level 1
70	How does it look and feel?	To use the appropriate vocabulary to describe materials.	Samples of the materials should be on hand for experiential purposes. Avoid glass containers – windows can be touched instead.	Science NC: Sc3 Grouping materials QCA: Unit 1C Sorting and using materials	SCN 013X – Properties and uses	AT1 Level 1 AT3 Level 1

Page	Activity	Objectives	Teachers' notes	NC, QCA & Primary Framework	Curriculum for Excellence (Scotland)	AT links and levels
71	What's it like?	To use appropriate vocabulary to describe materials.	Children choose a real object from the classroom to draw and describe. The words at the bottom are only a prop for the uninspired.	Science NC: Sc3 Grouping materials QCA: Unit 1C Sorting and using materials	SCN 013X – Properties and uses	AT1 Level 1 AT3 Level 1/2
72	What could you use to…?	To explore which materials are suitable for particular purposes.	The sheet is self-explanatory. Useful follow-up is to ask what makes a particular material good for one job but not another.	Science NC: Sc3 Grouping materials QCA: Unit 1C Sorting and using materials	SCN 013X – Properties and uses	AT1 Level 1 AT3 Level 1/2
73	Light and dark	To learn that there are many sources of light.	This will work best as a group activity with lots of discussion.	Science NC: Sc4 Light and sound QCA: Unit 1D Light and dark	SCN 004E – Astronomy	AT1 Level 1 AT4 Level 1
74	Ways to move	To observe and describe different ways of moving.	Watch and discuss movement in PE and the playground before using this sheet.	Science NC: Sc4 Forces and motion QCA: 1E Pushes and pulls	SCN 007L; SCN 008L – Forces and motion	AT1 Level 1 AT4 Level 1
75	Push and pull	To begin to know that forces such as pushes and pulls can move objects.	Again it is a matter of discussion first. *Who or what is pushing or pulling?*	Science NC: Sc4 Forces and motion QCA: 1E Pushes and pulls	SCN 007L; SCN 008L – Forces and motion	AT1 Level 1 AT4 Level 1
76	Pushing and pulling at home	To identify things in the home that are moved by pushing or pulling.	Make sure that children recognise and know the words on the sheet. This activity is essentially about observation.	Science NC: Sc4 Forces and motion QCA: 1E Pushes and pulls	SCN 007L; SCN 008L – Forces and motion	AT1 Level 1 AT4 Level 1
77	What makes it move?	To ask questions about what is causing movement and to understand that it is not only ourselves that cause things to move.	Answers are: wind, water, wind, wind, breath.	Science NC: Sc4 Forces and motion QCA: 1E Pushes and pulls	SCN 007L – Forces and motion SCN 107F – Energy transfer	AT1 Level 1 AT4 Level 1
78	Watch out! Because…	To recognise hazards and risks to themselves from moving objects.	Cut out the labels first. When the sheet has been completed the children should be challenged to describe why there is a danger.	Science NC: Sc4 Forces and motion QCA: 1E Pushes and pulls	SCN 007L – Forces and motion SCN 010S – Using my senses	AT1 Level 1/2
79	Barmy band	To describe the way in which sounds are made by musical instruments.	Circle the animals playing their instruments correctly. Finally, complete the sheet according to the instructions on it.	Science NC: Sc4 Light and sound QCA: Unit 1F Sound and hearing	SCN 008L – Forces and motion SCN 012W – Sound	AT1 Level 1 AT4 Level 1
80	Loud or quiet?	To learn that there are many ways to describe sound.	Encourage the use of words that they think of themselves, as well as those on the sheet.	Science NC: Sc4 Light and sound QCA: Unit 1F Sound and hearing	SCN 012W – Sound	AT1 Level 1 AT4 Level 1
81	Sounds I can make	To begin to explore the sounds we can make ourselves.	At an appropriate time, ask the children to reproduce all the sounds illustrated on the sheet then complete the exercise as instructed.	Science NC: Sc4 Light and sound QCA: Unit 1F Sound and hearing	SCN 012W – Sound	AT1 Level 1 AT4 Level 1
82	Old and new	To identify the characteristic features of old and new objects.	No sheet can replace the experience of handling real objects so provide them if you can. Encourage the use of adjectives of their own choice in discussion afterwards.	History NC: Historical enquiry QCA: Unit 1 How are our toys different…?	SOC 002C – People, past events and societies	AT Level 1/2
83	Where people live	To understand that people live in different sorts of homes and to learn appropriate vocabulary for talking about homes.	Once again, it is the discussion that might accompany the use of this sheet that is most important.	History NC: Knowledge of people in the past QCA: Unit 2 What were homes like a long time ago?	SOC 002C; SOC 003F – People, past events and societies	AT Level 1/2
84	A house from the past	To identify the key features of a house built a long time ago.	Not an easy sheet to do without preparation. Look at photographs of similar houses; walk a street and discuss the features of houses that you see, then the activity can be tackled.	History NC: Knowledge of people in the past QCA: Unit 2 What were homes like a long time ago?	SOC 002C; SOC 003F – People, past events and societies	AT Level 1/2

Page	Activity	Objectives	Teachers' notes	NC, QCA & Primary Framework	Curriculum for Excellence (Scotland)	AT links and levels
85	Household objects from a long time ago	To recognise household objects from a long time ago and to make inferences from them about aspects of home life in the past.	This sheet works best if used in conjunction with a collection of artefacts provided by a friendly museum or another suitable source.	History NC: Knowledge of people in the past QCA: Unit 2 What were homes like a long time ago?	SOC 002C – People, past events and societies	AT Level 1/2
86	Home life	To recognise household objects from a long time ago and to make inferences from them about aspects of home life in the past.	Children must describe what they see, then they can engage in detective work. *How does it work? What could it be used for ?* and so on.	History NC: Knowledge of people in the past QCA: Unit 2 What were homes like a long time ago?	SOC 002C – People, past events and societies	AT Level 1/2
87	What has changed?	To make inferences about life a long time ago and to spot changes between now and then.	This is clearly a sheet for talking about. The answers may be obvious but the reasons for those answers need drawing out. The pictures can be cut out, stuck in books and written about.	History NC: Historical enquiry; Knowledge about people and changes in the past QCA: Unit 2 What were homes like a long time ago?	SOC 002C; SOC 103C – People, past events and societies	AT Level 1/2
88	Going to school	To carry out a survey of how children travel to school and learn how to represent this as a simple graph.	This can be done as a group activity. The 'stickers' can be duplicated if required. Explain how to construct a graph as necessary.	Geography NC: Geographical enquiry and skills QCA: Unit 1 Around our school	SOC 005G – People, place and environment	AT Level 1
89	On the way to school	To recognise some of the physical features of their locality.	Talk first about the journeys that the class make in order to get to school; the imaginary journey on the sheet can follow.	Geography NC: Knowledge and understanding of places QCA: Unit 1 Around our school	SOC 005G; SOC 003F – People, place and environment	AT Level 1
90	Where I live	To understand that we all have a personal address and what this address means.	This sheet is an excuse for discussing addresses. *What does each line of the school address mean? How does it help people to find the school?* The sheet will need to be read to less confident readers.	Geography NC: Knowledge and understanding of places QCA: Unit 1 Around our school		AT Level 1
91	Nice and nasty	To begin to use a range of words and pictures to describe the quality of the environment.	Discuss what makes a place 'nice' or 'nasty'. Assist children to express and record their views.	Geography NC: Knowledge and understanding of environmental change and sustainable development QCA: Unit 1 Around our school	SOC 003F; SOC 105F; SOC 106G – People, place and environment	AT Level 1/2
92	Leisure tally	To understand about leisure and its need for special facilities. To learn how to tally.	Thoroughly practise the technique of tallying. The target group for the survey has deliberately been left open.	Geography NC: Geographical enquiry and skills; Knowledge and understanding of places QCA: Unit 1 Around our school	SOC 118R – People, place and environment	AT Level 1/2
93	Making safe	To understand that places can be made safer or better.	Four choices only! Children can be led to understand that you can rarely have everything that you want.	Geography NC: Knowledge and understanding of environmental change and sustainable development QCA: Unit 1 Around our school	SOC 106G – People, place and environment	AT Level 1/2
94	Traffic count	To ask questions about roads and traffic and to collect data and display it in graphical form.	This may require a supervised trip out of the classroom (unless you have well-placed windows). A quiet street is best. Mark each vehicle by using a dot initially; you can decide how to deal with the results back in the classroom. The survey must be strictly time-limited.	Geography NC: Geographical enquiry and skills QCA: Unit 1 Around our school	SOC 005G – People, place and environment	AT Level 1/2
95	Moving Ted	To make a simple moving mechanism.	Ted must be mounted onto card. More dextrous children might cut Ted out for themselves. Discuss how to make the limbs move: there is more than one way of doing this.	Design and technology NC: Working with tools, equipment, materials and components to make quality products; Knowledge and understanding of materials and components QCA: Unit 1A Moving pictures	TCH 003C; TCH 105C – Technologies	AT Level 1/2
96	See-saw	To suggest an idea and explain what they are going to do (to make a simple lever mechanism).	Stick the see-saw onto card. This is problem solving so the items in the box are only there as suggestions.	Design and technology NC: Developing, planning and communicating ideas QCA: Unit 1A Moving pictures	TCH 003C; TCH 105C – Technologies	AT Level 1/2

Page	Activity	Objectives	Teachers' notes	NC, QCA & Primary Framework	Curriculum for Excellence (Scotland)	AT links and levels
97	Fruit and vegetables	To understand that there are many fruits and vegetables and that they have separate names. To understand basic practices in food handling.	The fruits and vegetables can be named orally using the names at the bottom of the sheet. Discuss why we wash and peel.	Design and technology NC: Breadth of study QCA: Unit 1C Eat more fruit and vegetables	TCH 005DC – Technologies	AT Level 1
98	Houses can be different	To observe that people live in different homes around the world and that there are reasons for the differences.	Investigate the pictures of houses with the children and discuss what they are made from and why in each case.	Design and technology NC: Evaluating processes and products QCA: Unit 1D Homes	TCH 004D;TCH 005D – Technologies	AT Level 1
99	Playtime	To investigate items of equipment found in a playground, to think about what they are made from and how they are put together. To design and build a model swing.	The construction exercise suggested on this sheet will clearly demand preparation and the provision of materials and equipment.	Design and technology NC: Evaluating products; Working with tools, equipment, materials and components to produce quality products QCA: Unit 1B Playgrounds	TCH 004D;TCH 105C – Technologies	AT Level 1/2
100	Reading pictures	To understand that pictures provide information and that computers use icons to provide information and instructions.	Tell the children that they need to read the pictures and say what information they convey to us. Can the children give any reasons as to why pictures are used instead of words? Introduce the term 'icon'.	ICT NC: Exchanging and sharing information QCA: Unit 1C The information around us	TCH 112H – Technologies	AT Level 1
101	Icon chart	To understand that pictures provide information and that computers use icons to provide information and instructions.	This sheet requires access to a computer.	ICT NC: Exchanging and sharing information QCA: Unit 1C The information around us	TCH 112H – Technologies	AT Level 1
102	Sorting animals	To understand that objects can be divided according to criteria.	How the animals are shown in the correct sets is a matter of choice depending on the ability of the child.	ICT NC: Exchanging and sharing information QCA: Unit 1D Labelling and classifying	TCH 115K – Technologies	AT Level 1/2
103	Favourite colours	To realise that ICT can be used to collect data and record a simple pictogram.	If this small survey requires more paper simply duplicate. Investigate the results as a whole-class exercise.	ICT NC: Finding things out QCA: Unit 1E Representing data graphically	TCH 115K – Technologies	AT Level 1/2
104	Push, pull or twist	To recognise that machines and devices must be controlled.	A practical demonstration of these modes of operation would make the sheet both easier and more relevant.	ICT NC: Breadth of study QCA: Unit 1F Understanding instructions…	TCH 114J;TCH 115K – Technologies	AT Level 1
105	A portrait (1)	To focus attention on portraits.	Introduce the word 'portrait'. Lead the class in how to read a picture by interrogating one that they can see in the school.	Art and design NC: Evaluating and developing work QCA: Unit 1A Self-portrait	EXA 005E – Art and design	AT Level 1
106	A portrait (2)	To focus attention on portraits.	Approach this activity in the same manner as the previous sheet.	Art and design NC: Evaluating and developing work QCA: Unit 1A Self-portrait	EXA 005E – Art and design	AT Level 1
107	In the mirror	To record self-portraits from observation.	A mirror is required by the child undertaking this exercise. This is all about observation.	Art and design NC: Evaluating and developing work QCA: Unit 1A Self-portrait	EXA 005E; EXA 006H – Art and design	AT Level 1
108	Spot the fabric	To understand what is meant by a fabric.	Draw connecting lines to the objects from the words. 'Fabric' is the root of the word 'fabrication' and applies to something made.	Art and design NC: Knowledge and understanding QCA: Unit 1B Investigating materials	EXA 003C; EXA 004D – Art and design	AT Level 2
109	Sculpture	To understand what a sculpture is and to make comments about a work of sculpture.	Introduce the word 'sculpture'. Talk about materials used by sculptors. Make similar sculptures in clay if this is possible.	Art and design NC: Knowledge and understanding QCA: Unit 1C What is sculpture?	EXA 005E; EXA 105E – Art and design	AT Level 1/2

Page	Activity	Objectives	Teachers' notes	NC, QCA & Primary Framework	Curriculum for Excellence (Scotland)	AT links and levels
110	Little Red Riding Hood	To use their voices in different ways, for example singing and whispering.	A group of eight is ideal for this activity (it's not much fun on your own). A different voice must be used for each character.	Music NC: Controlling sounds through singing and playing QCA: Unit 2 Sounds interesting	EXA 011Q – Music EXA 111M – Drama	AT Level 1
111	Making sounds	To explore different sounds that can be made using hands, feet, mouth and so on.	Whole-class involvement is best for sanity's sake. You might lead by describing what is in the picture as the class makes the appropriate sounds.	Music NC: Controlling sounds through singing and playing QCA: Unit 2 Sounds interesting	EXA 011Q – Music	AT Level 1
112	Long and short sounds	To explore duration and to use their voices to make long and short sounds.	Note that the words are given in the order of the illustrations within each pair.	Music NC: Controlling sounds through singing and playing; Listening and applying knowledge and understanding QCA: Unit 3 The long and short of it	EXA 011Q; EXA 113Q – Music	AT Level 1
113	Higher and lower	To follow pitch movement and to sing, moving up or down, following changes in pitch.	This needs a little practice; try some examples of your own first. Encourage children to sing the tunes in their heads.	Music NC: Controlling sounds through singing and playing – performing skills; Listening and applying knowledge and understanding QCA: Unit 5 Taking off	EXA 011Q; EXA 113Q – Music	AT Level 1/2
114	Belonging	To identify ways in which they belong and to consolidate their understanding of the world.	Explain the sheet and get the children to fill in their surnames or family names as indicated. The words at the bottom are suggestions only.	RE Non-statutory framework: Breadth of study (Themes) QCA: Unit 1A What does it mean to belong?		Non-statutory AT2 Level 1
115	Belonging: religion (1)	To understand that religious people belong to a faith and to identify some of the ways in which this belonging is identified.	Belonging to a faith community is treated as an extension to the idea of belonging to a family. Knowledge is required to complete the sheet so it must be used after appropriate preparation. Answers are: font, church and cross for Christianity; Magen David (Star of David), kippah (skull cap) and menorah (candlestick) for Judaism.	RE Non-statutory framework: Learning about religion; Breadth of study (Religions and beliefs) QCA: Unit 1A What does it mean to belong? Unit 1D Beliefs and practice		Non-statutory AT1 Level 1
116	Belonging: religion (2)	To understand that religious people belong to a faith and to identify some of the ways in which this belonging is identified.	Use as above. Answers are: hijab, mosque, star and crescent moon and prayer cap for Islam; aum symbol and mandir (temple) for Hinduism.	RE Non-statutory framework: Learning about religion; Breadth of study (Religions and beliefs) QCA: Unit 1A What does it mean to belong? Unit 1D Beliefs and practice		Non-statutory AT1 Level 1
117	Belonging: religion (3)	To understand that religious people belong to a faith and to identify some of the ways in which this belonging is identified.	Answers are: Gurdwara (place of worship), kangha (special comb) and kara (steel bracelet) for Sikhism; lotus flower, eight-spoked Dhamma wheel and Buddha for Buddhism.	RE Non-statutory framework: Learning about religion; Breadth of study (Religions and beliefs) QCA: Unit 1A What does it mean to belong? Unit 1D Beliefs and practice		Non-statutory AT1 Level 1
118	Christmas gifts	To know the Christmas story and to understand why Christians give gifts at Christmas.	Mount the pictures onto card. Challenge the children to arrange the pictures in the correct order of events. Draw in the blank as required (a suitable present for Jesus perhaps).	RE Non-statutory framework: Learning about religion; Breadth of study (Religions and beliefs) QCA: Unit 1C Celebrations		Non-statutory AT1Level 1/2
119	Belonging: Christianity	To recognise ways in which belonging to Christianity is demonstrated and to learn that baptism is the way that some Christians welcome babies into the family of Jesus.	*How do we show we belong?* The blanks at the bottom relate to belonging to a school as shown by the wearing of a badge or a uniform.	RE Non-statutory framework: Learning about religion; Breadth of study (Religions and beliefs) QCA: Unit 1B What does it mean to belong?		Non-statutory AT1 Level 1/2
120	Welcome to our school	To observe the local environment and to say how it might be improved.	This needs explanation and discussion – and a visit to the school entrance. Discuss what makes a visitor feel welcome.	PSHE and Citizenship NC guidelines: Preparing to play an active role as citizens QCA: Unit 1 Taking part		N/A

Page	Activity	Objectives	Teachers' notes	NC, QCA & Primary Framework	Curriculum for Excellence (Scotland)	AT links and levels
121	Good things about my friend	To develop confidence in expressing opinions about things that matter to them.	Encourage positive thinking and moving beyond the superficial and trivial observation.	PSHE and Citizenship NC guidelines: Developing confidence and responsibility QCA: Unit 1 Taking part		N/A
122	Keeping safe in school	To make safe choices based on right/wrong and good/bad.	Discussion is required here. The 'don'ts' must link to consequences – not simply 'because my mum says so'.	PSHE and Citizenship NC guidelines: Developing a healthy, safer lifestyle QCA: Unit 2 Choices		N/A
123	Moving house	To recognise and name feelings – those associated with change.	Talk about moving house: *Has anyone done this recently? How did you feel?* Explain how people have different feelings for a number of reasons. The word 'because' is the link word here.	PSHE and Citizenship NC guidelines: Developing confidence and responsibility QCA: Unit 1 Taking part		N/A
124	Permission	To learn to ask for and to give permission. To listen to other people and play and work cooperatively.	Mount the wheels onto card. Fasten the small wheel to the centre of the large one. Working in groups, children rotate the wheel to generate questions. The group decides on an answer but must give a reason. Adult intervention is ideal at this point. The adult may play devil's advocate.	PSHE and Citizenship NC guidelines: Preparing to play an active role as citizens QCA: Unit 1 Taking part		N/A
125	I am good at…	To develop confidence by recognising what they are good at.	Discuss, but be positive – focus on skills not weaknesses. Choose only three stamps.	PSHE and Citizenship NC guidelines: Developing confidence and responsibility QCA: Unit 1 Taking part		N/A
126	Mistakes	To learn from their experiences and know that it is all right to make mistakes. To learn how their behaviour affects others.	It is easy to tick boxes but the value must lie in the talk about the mistakes: treading on a cat is regrettable but all right if it is accidental – mistakes are allowed.	PSHE and Citizenship NC guidelines: Developing good relationships and respecting the differences between people QCA: Unit 1 Taking part		N/A
127	Feelings	To recognise and name feelings.	Acceptable alternatives to the words provided are allowed. An adult might be used to write down words thought of by the children as description should not be limited by the child's spelling ability. You could introduce the children to a simple thesaurus.	PSHE and Citizenship NC guidelines: Developing confidence and responsibility QCA: Unit 1 Taking part		N/A

Name ______________________

Rhyme and count

Complete the rhymes. Then cut them out and put them in the right order.

One, two,
Buckle my ______________.

Nine, ten,
A big fat ______________.

Five, six,
Pick up ______________.

Three, four,
Knock at the ______________.

Seven, eight,
Lay them ______________.

door

shoe

hen

sticks

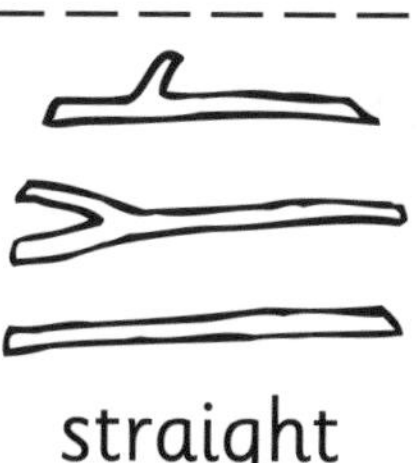
straight

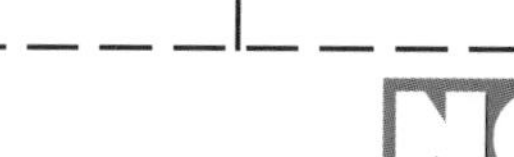

Name ______________________

Nobody spoke

- Fill in the rhymes with the words from the right.

I went to Noke

But nobody ____________.

I went to Slad

It was just as ____________.

Batley and Brill

Were silent and ____________.

But I went to Tring

And they started to ____________.

still

sing

spoke

bad

- Use the letters to make some new rhymes.

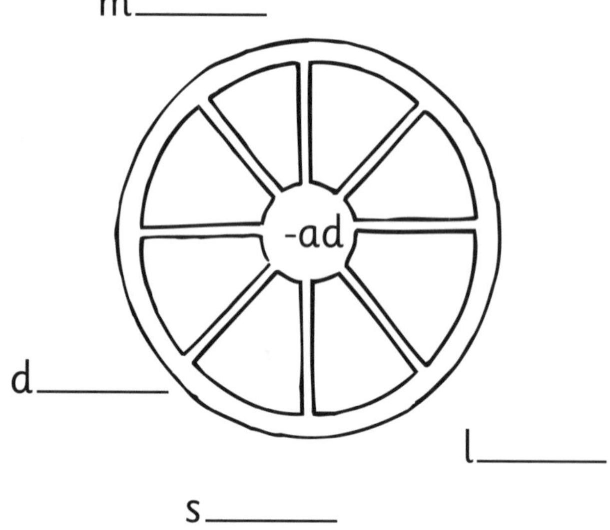

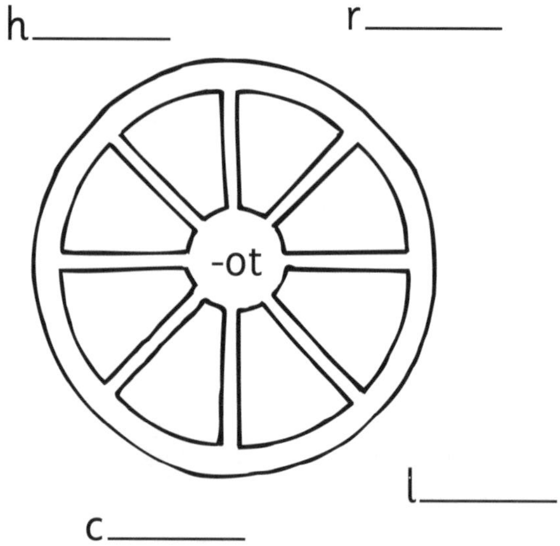

Name ______________________________

Rhyme lines

Hang the shirts from the basket on the right line.

Name ______________________

Lewis' ladder game

Change **one** letter at a time. Can you make **dog** into **cat**?

Name ________________________________

Word factory

Put together beginnings and endings. How many words can you make? Write them in the box below.

Name ____________________

Spelling bee

Use the endings in the centre of the flowers to make as many words as you can.

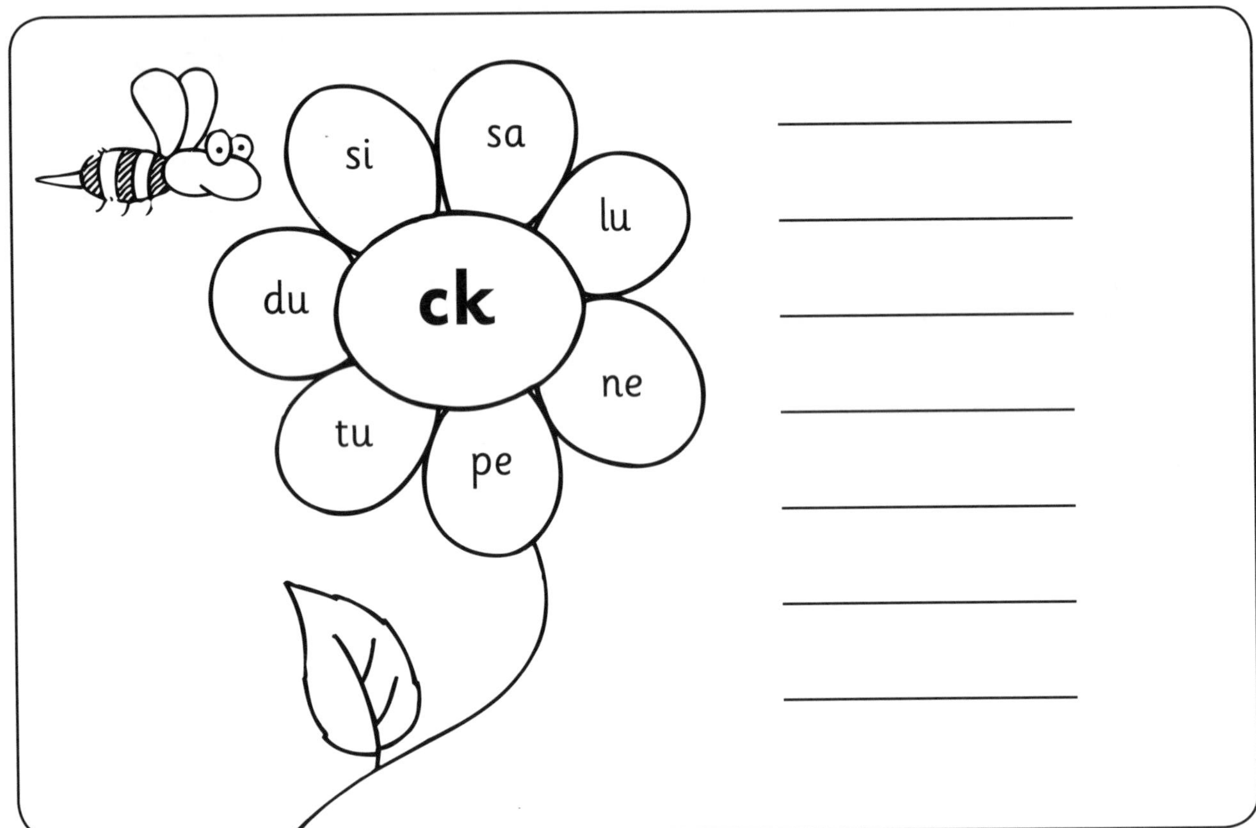

ha
si
lu
ng
ra
ba
wi
lo

SCHOLASTIC
www.scholastic.co.uk

Name ______________________________

Word slide

Cut out the two strips. Slide the two strips to make as many words as you can.

br	
bl	
cl	
cr	an
dr	ow
gl	aw
gr	ate
pl	ip
sk	ot
st	ick
tr	ill

Name ____________________

Beginnings

Use these beginnings to finish the words. fl fr sn spr

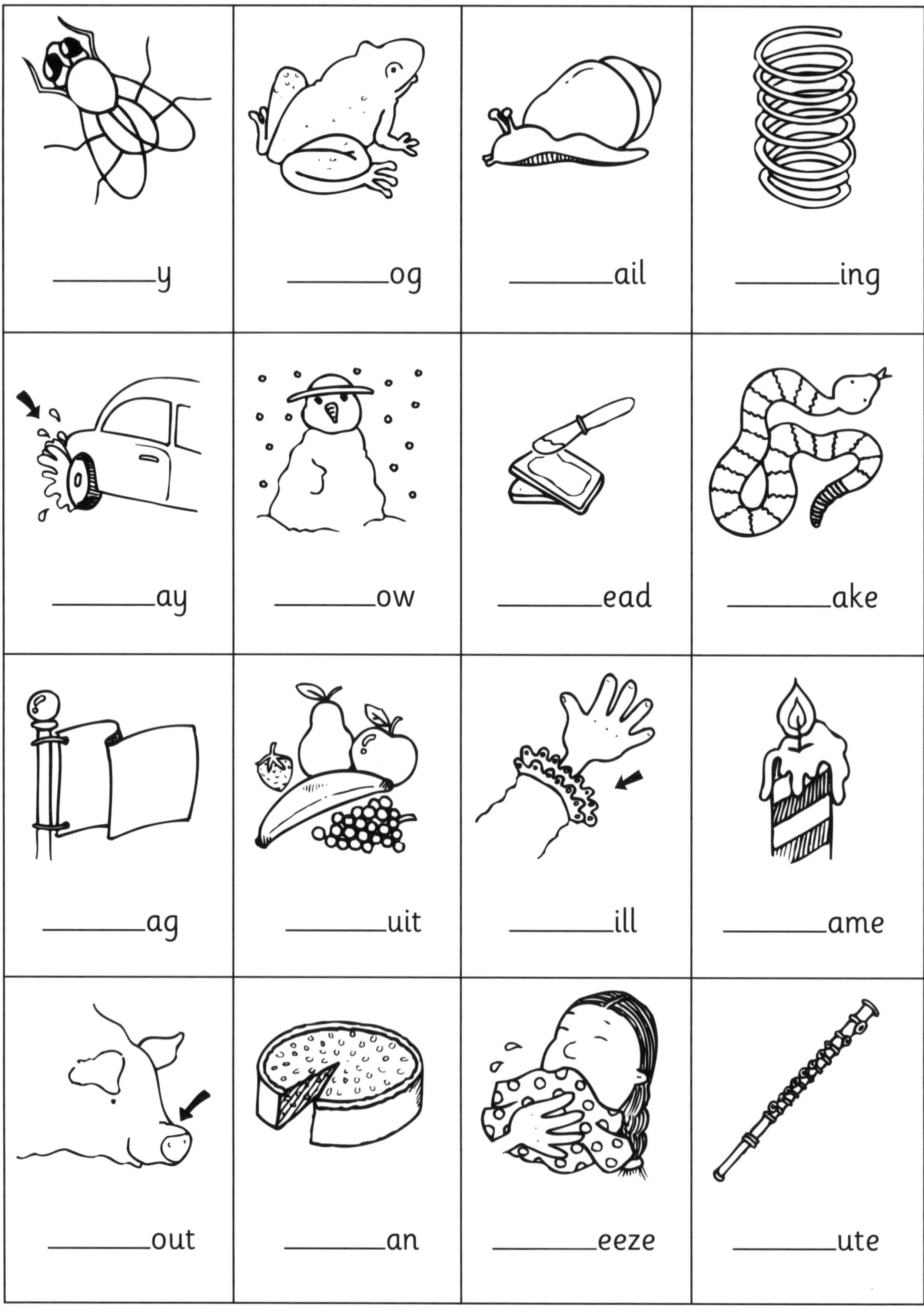

______y	______og	______ail	______ing
______ay	______ow	______ead	______ake
______ag	______uit	______ill	______ame
______out	______an	______eeze	______ute

Name ___________________________________

Finish the job (1)

Use these endings to finish the words. (ld nd lk nk)

 co______	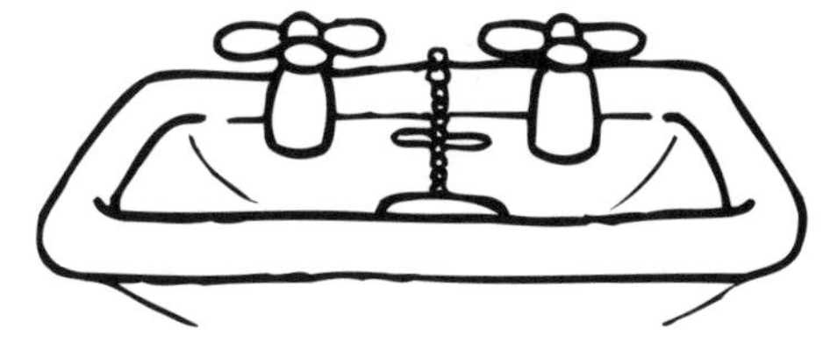 si______
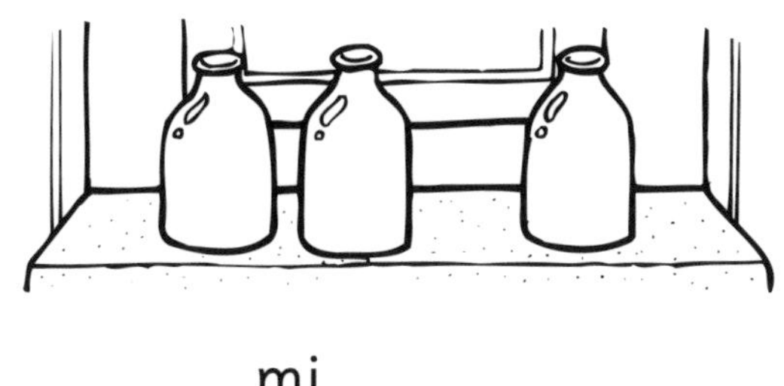 mi______	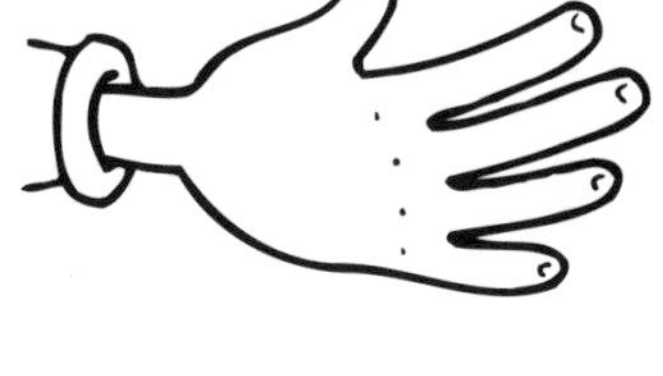 ha______
 ta______	 fie______
 sa______	 li______
 po______	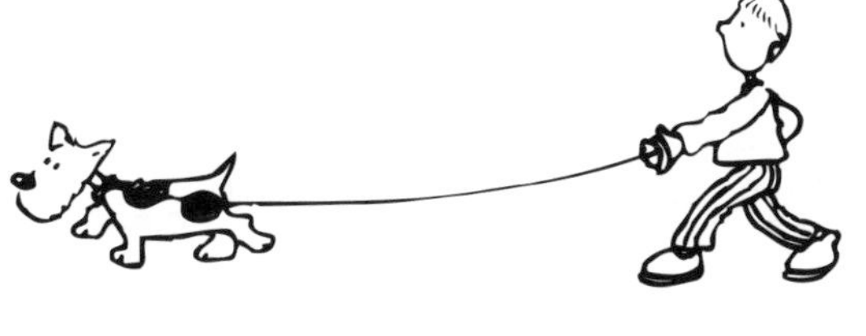 wa______

Name ______________________

Finish the job (2)

Use these endings to finish the words. (st nch mp sk)

 de______	 bu______	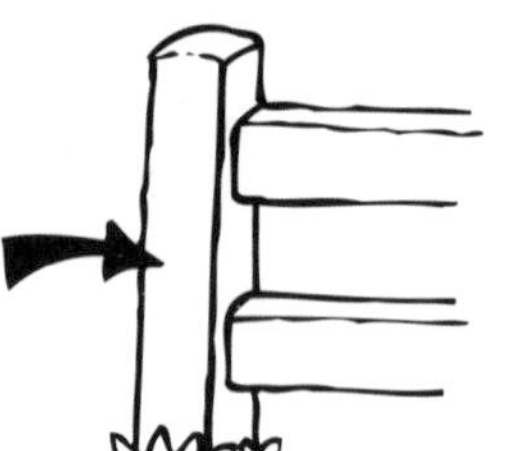 po______	 la______
 ma______	 li______	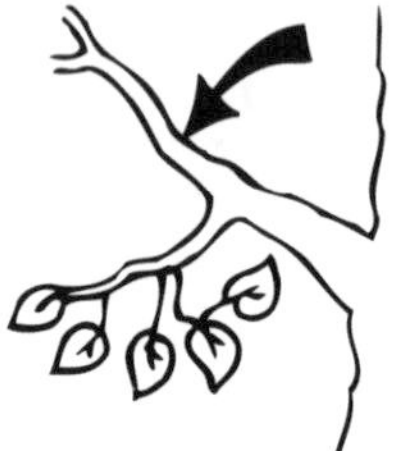 bra______	 sta______
 li______	 coa______	 mi______	 lu______
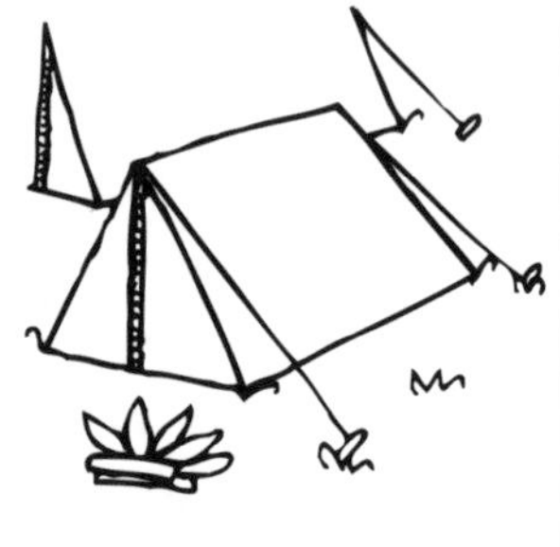 ca______	 fla______	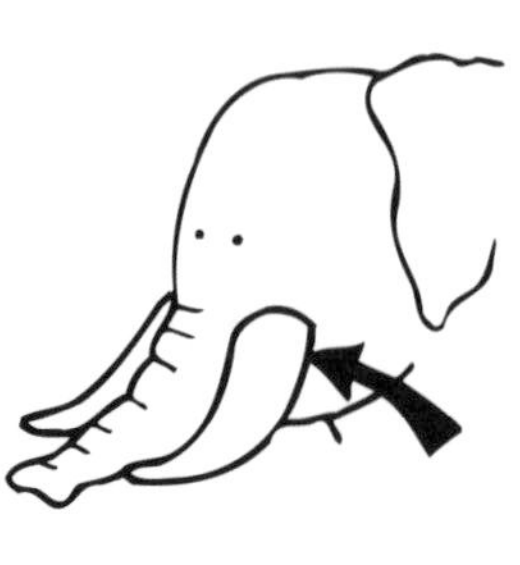 tu______	 pu______

Name ______________________________

Say and spell: 'ea' in seat

- Say and spell the words below.

s 

t 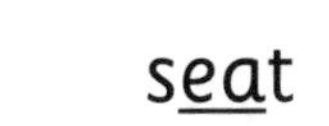

n 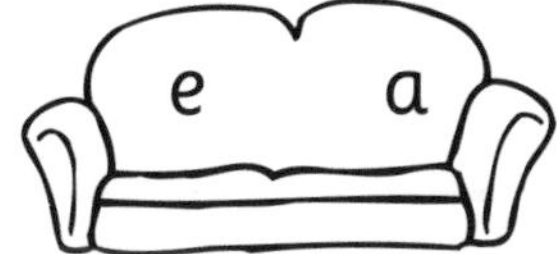

t 

h 

t 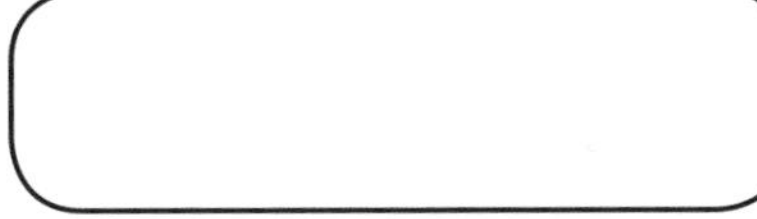

b 

t 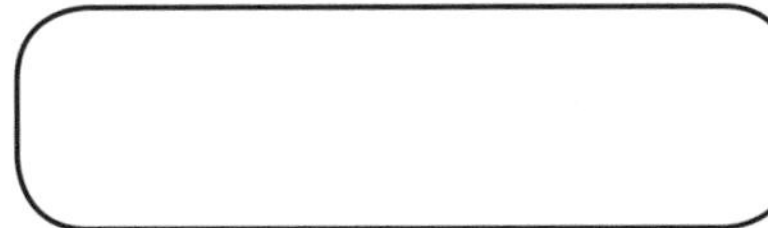

l 

p 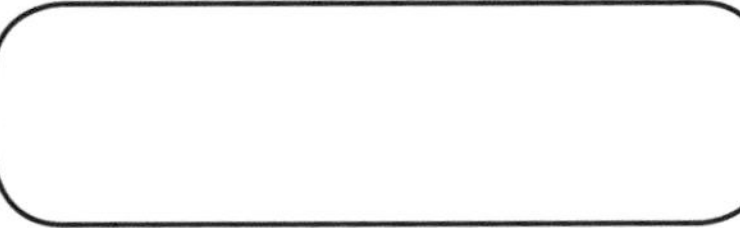

m 

t 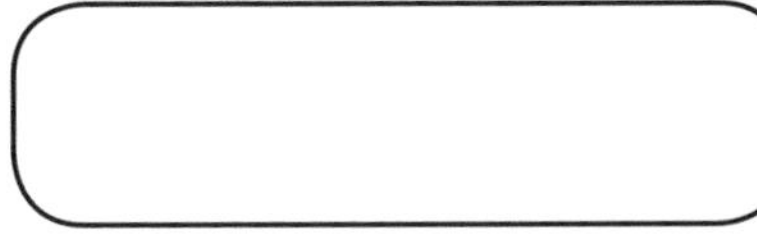

- Can you make any more 'ea' words?

Name ____________________

Say and spell: 'ee' in weep

- Say and spell the words below.

w	e	e	p	weep
d	e	e	p	
k	e	e	p	
f	e	e	l	
s	e	e	d	
m	e	e	t	

- Can you make any more 'ee' words?

Name ____________________________

Say and spell: 'ai' in paid

- Say and spell the words below.

p	a i	d	paid
r	a i	d	
w	a i	t	
tr	a i	n	
st	a i	n	
l	a i	d	

- Can you make any more 'ai' words?

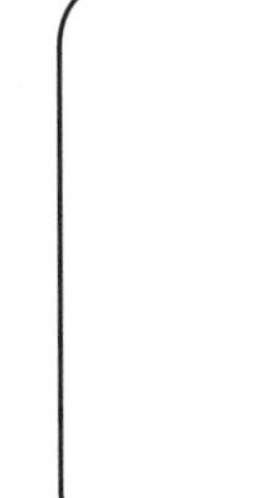

Name ______________________

Say and spell: 'igh' in light

- Say and spell the words below.

l	igh	t	light
t	igh	t	
s	igh		
br	igh	t	
h	igh		
f	igh	t	

- Can you make any more 'igh' words?

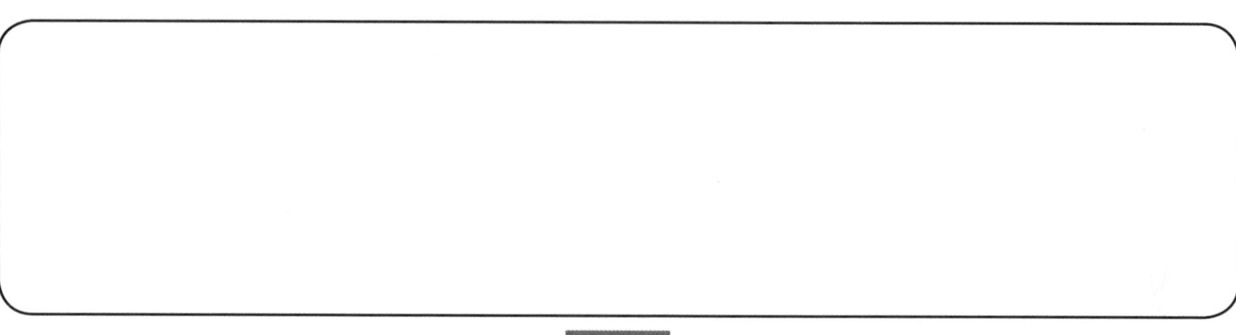

SCHOLASTIC www.scholastic.co.uk

Name ______________________________

Say and spell: 'oa' in boat

- Say and spell the words below.

b  oa t  boat

c oa t 

l  oa d

t oa d 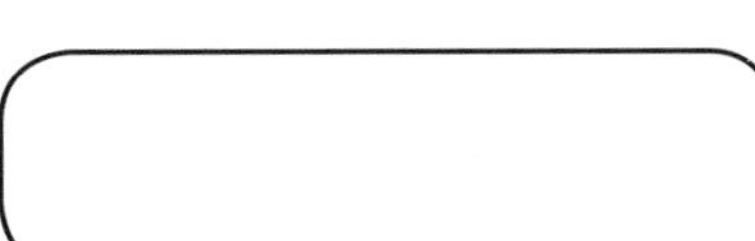

s oa p 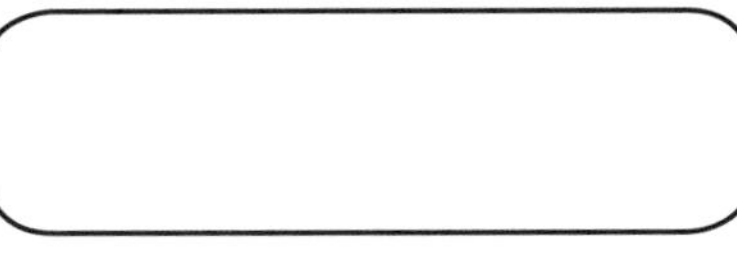

r  oa d 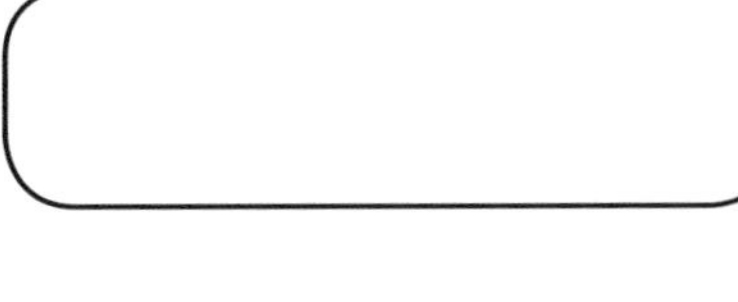

- Can you make any more 'oa' words?

Name ______________________

Say and spell: 'oo' in hoot

- Say and spell the words below.

h  t

hoot

b  t 

sh  t 

m  n 

r  m 

- Can you make any more 'oo' words?

Name ______________________________

Dream sentences

Colour in the sentences that make sense.

Name ______________________________

Build brick sentences

Colour a brick in each pile to make a sentence.

Sarah	ran	to	my	table.
I	fell	for	a	mum.
They	ate	by	his	bed.
Dan	jumped	down	the	shop.
He	slept	on	her	box.
She	sang	over	their	stairs.

Name ______________________

Say and write: same sounds

Complete the words.

a–e came	 g______	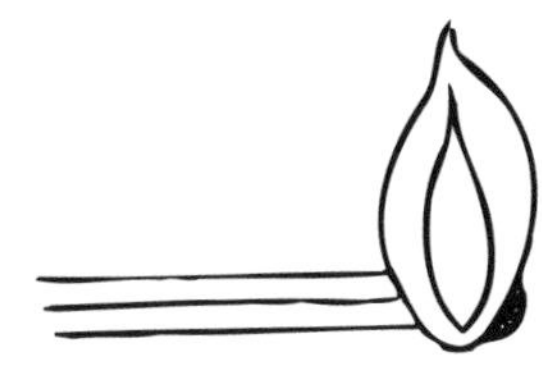 fl______	 n______
i–e white	 k______	 b______	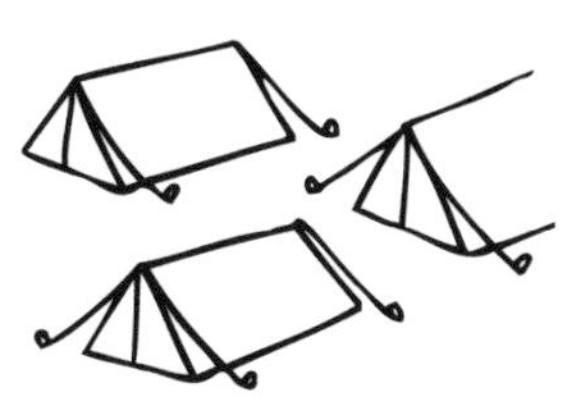 s______
o–e vole	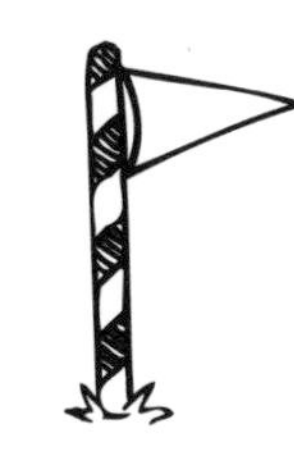 p______	 h______	 m______
u–e June	 t______	 pr______	 d______

Name ____________________

Capital beginnings

Choose the capital letter to begin these sentences.

☐ live in a house.

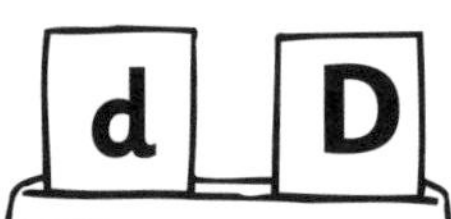

☐ aisy lives in a flat.

☐ am lives in a caravan.

☐ y dog bites.

☐ lost my tooth.

☐ an I play?

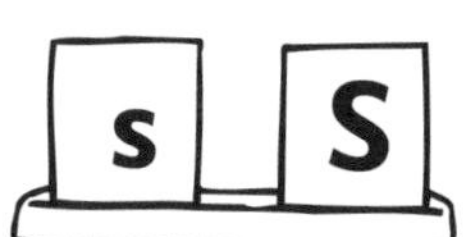

☐ ally had a bath.

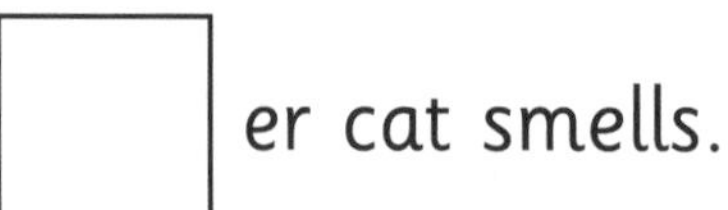

☐ er cat smells.

Name ___________________

Missing titles

Write these titles on the books correctly. Don't forget capital letters.

paddington bear

little miss muffet

harry's mad

when the wind blows

mr tick the teacher

little red riding hood

Name ______________________________

Hands up!

Put question marks only after the questions.

Name ________________________________

Story sense

Cut out the sentences and put them in the best order to make sense.

She walked home with the pail of milk.

Mary milked the cow.

Moo! The cow waited to be milked in the shed.

The cat drank the milk.

Mary poured some milk into a saucer.

The cat saw her coming.

Name ______________________________

Rick Wrong and Rose Right

What would Rose write? Write the correct sentences.

my shoes put I on.	Rick
I put my shoes on.	Rose
my bed makes My mum for me.	Rick
	Rose
my boots ate Fido.	Rick
	Rose
going Are school to you?	Rick
	Rose
the TV sat on Dad it broke and.	Rick
	Rose
the bath sings in Aunt Jean.	Rick
	Rose
down Sit to lunch your eat.	Rick
	Rose

www.scholastic.co.uk

Name ____________________

Football numbers

- Fill in the missing shirt numbers. Which is the number 9 shirt?

- How many boots are there?

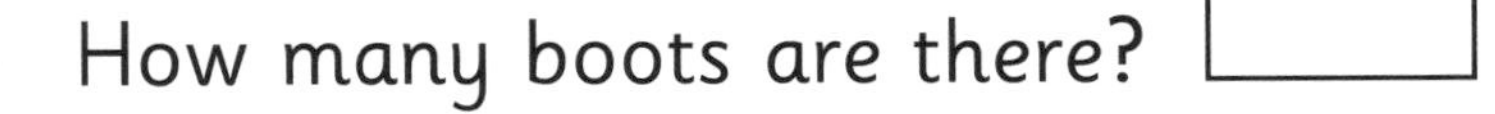

Name ____________________

Jumping in tens

Complete the jumps for the animals by filling in the numbers.

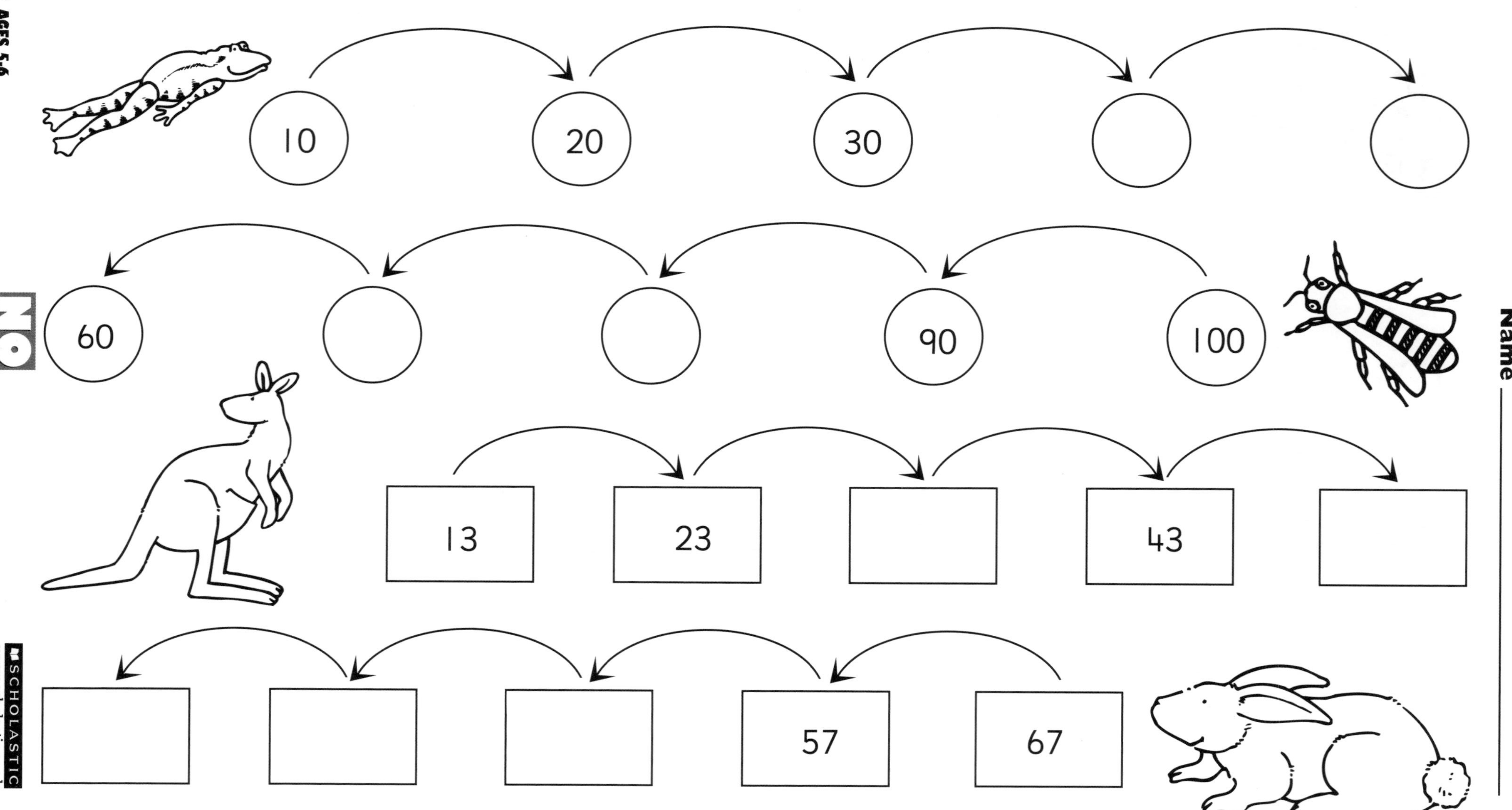

SCHOLASTIC www.scholastic.co.uk

Name ____________________

Odds and evens

- Colour every other number. Start with **1**.

1	2	3	4	5	6	7	8	9	10	11	12	13	14	15	16	17	18	19	20

- Colour every other number. Start with **2**.

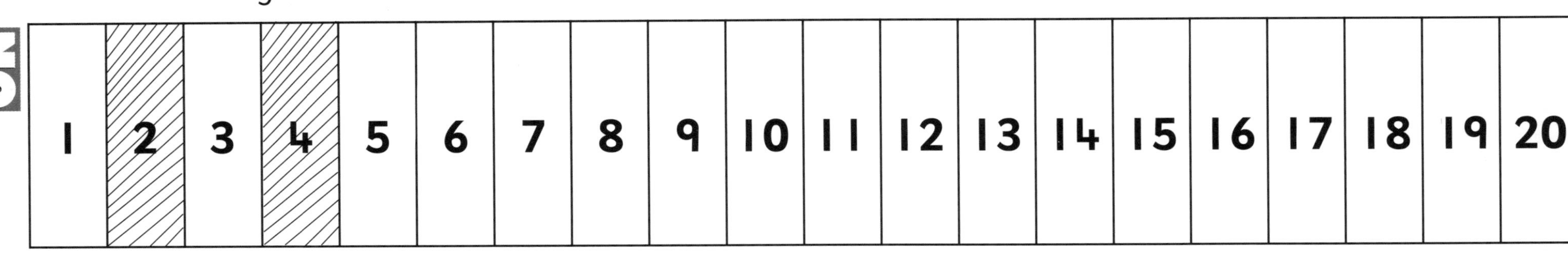

1	2	3	4	5	6	7	8	9	10	11	12	13	14	15	16	17	18	19	20

- Which numbers come next?

10, 12, 14, 16, 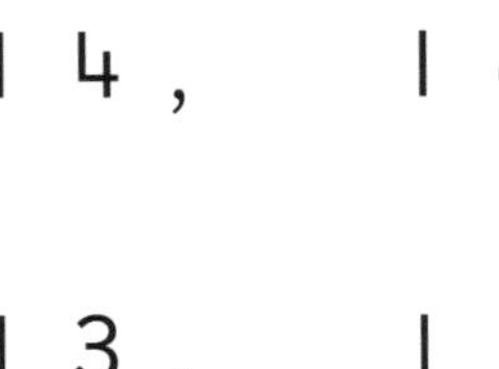, 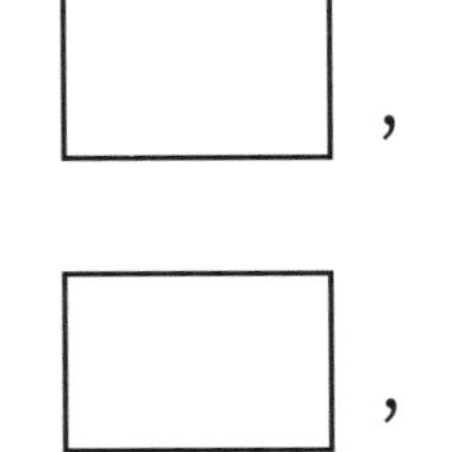, 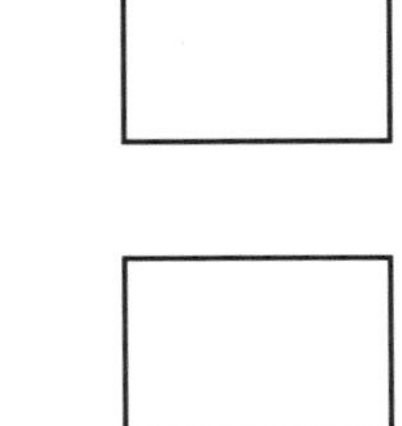

17, 15, 13, 11, 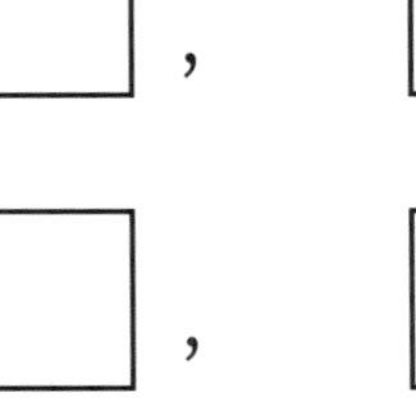, 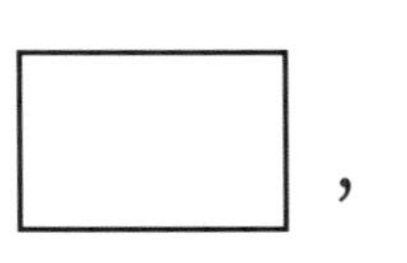, 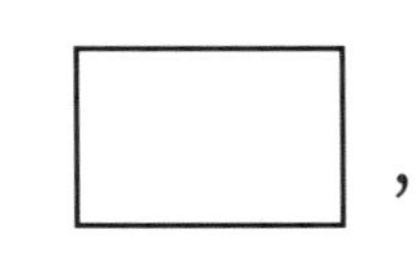

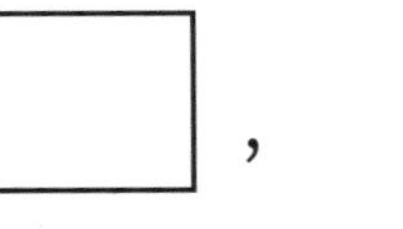
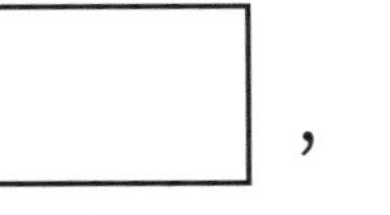
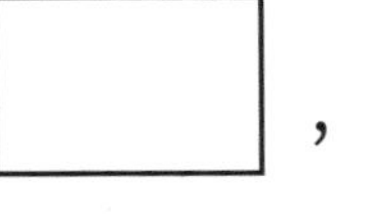
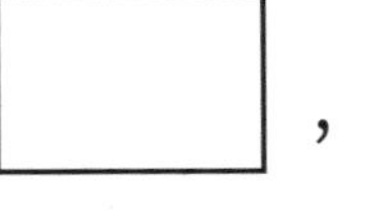
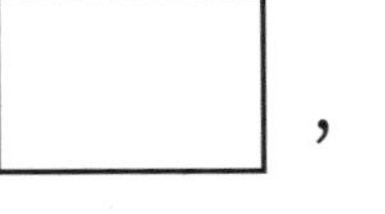
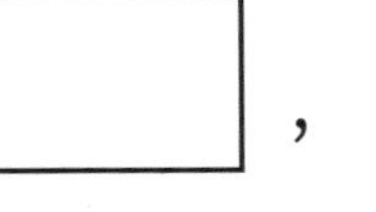
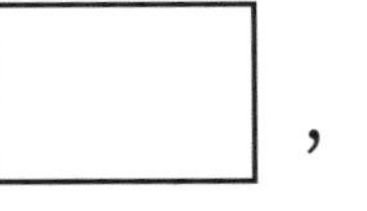

Name ______________________________

Missing numbers

Finish the number sequences by filling in the blanks.

5, 10, 15, ☐, ☐

2, 4, 6, ☐, ☐

3, 6, 9, ☐, ☐

2, 4, 6, ☐, 10, ☐

10, 15, ☐, 25, ☐, ☐

3, 6, ☐, 12, ☐, ☐

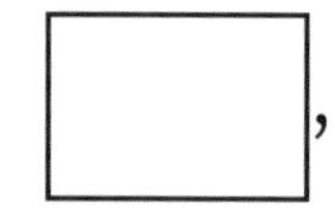

30, 25, ☐, 15, ☐, ☐

22, 20, ☐, 16, ☐, ☐

0 1 2 3 4 5 6 7 8 9 10 11 12 13 14 15 16 17 18 19 20 21 22 23 24 25

SCHOLASTIC www.scholastic.co.uk

Name ______________________________

Writing numbers

Fill in the gaps with numerals or words.

→ 15 → fifteen

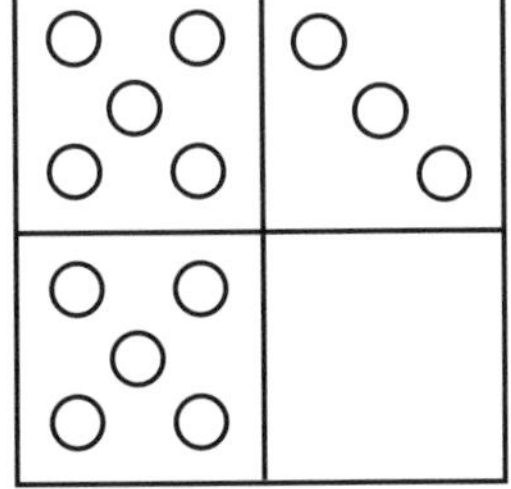

→ 13 →

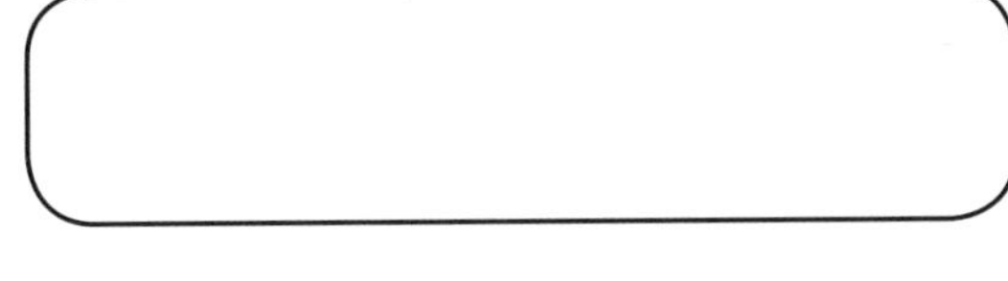

→ ☐ → eleven

→ 19 → ☐

→ 16 → ☐

thirteen	sixteen	nineteen
eleven	fifteen	seventeen

Name ______________________

Tens and ones

Write down how many tens and ones are on the abacus.

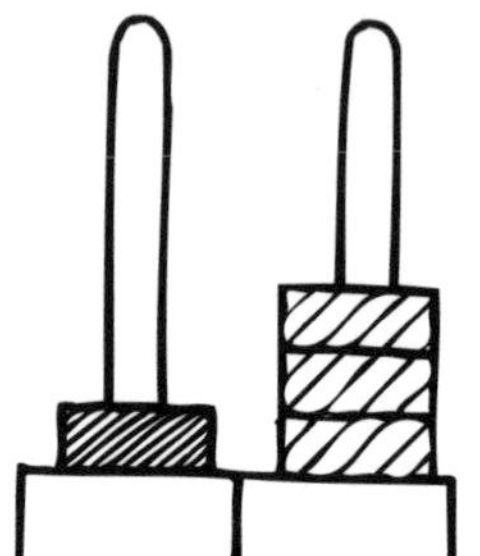

→ 1 ten 3 ones → 13

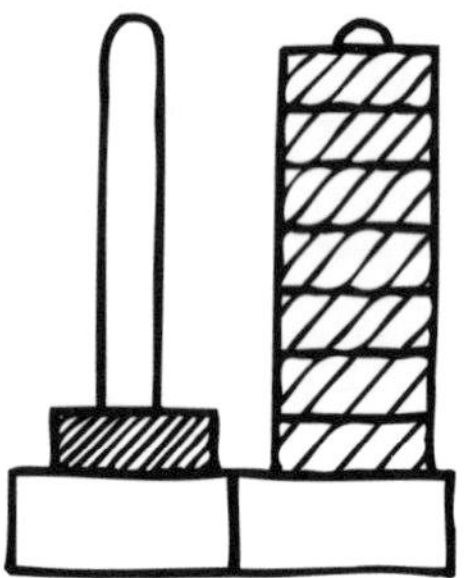

→ ☐ ten ☐ ones → ☐

→ ☐ ten ☐ ones → ☐

→ ☐ ten ☐ ones → ☐

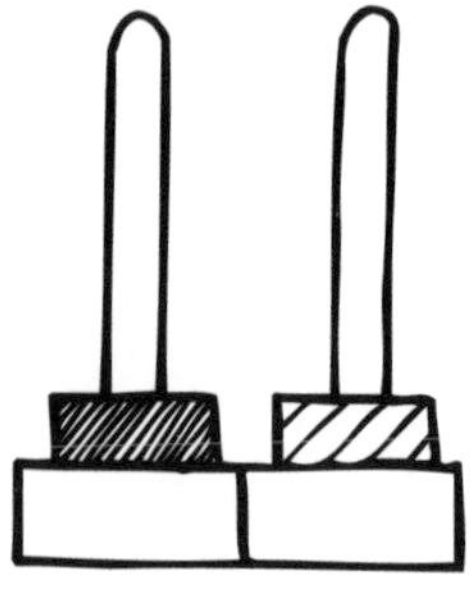

→ ☐ ten ☐ one → ☐

Name ______________________

More tens and ones

Write down how many tens and ones make up these numbers.

13	→	1	ten	3	ones
10	→		ten		ones
19	→		ten		ones
11	→		ten		one
20	→		tens		ones
16	→		ten		ones
12	→		ten		ones
18	→		ten		ones
17	→		ten		ones
15	→		ten		ones
14	→		ten		ones

Name ___________________________

Number splits

Split the numbers by filling in the boxes.

14 = ☐ + ☐

12 = ☐ + 2

17 = 10 + ☐

13 = ☐ + 3

18 = ☐ + 8

10 = 10 + ☐

23 = 20 + ☐

28 = ☐ + 8

35 = ☐ + 5

47 = 40 + ☐

SCHOLASTIC
www.scholastic.co.uk

Name ____________________

In the queue

- Who comes where in the queue?

Elephant is [ ] in the queue.

Mouse is [ ] in the queue.

Ostrich is [ ] in the queue.

Pig is [ ] in the queue.

Giraffe is [ ] in the queue.

- Who is last in the queue? ____________________

Name ______________________

More than...

One more than 6 is 7

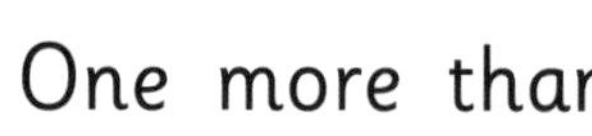
One more than 4 is

One more than 9 is

One more than 13 is

One more than 19 is

One more than 24 is

One more than 16 is

One more than 12 is

One more than 25 is

One more than 27 is

One more than 18 is

Name ______________________________

Less than...

One less than 7 is [6]

One less than 17 is [ ]

One less than 24 is [ ]

One less than 4 is [ ]

One less than 28 is 

One less than 8 is 

One less than 30 is [ ]

One less than 25 is [ ]

One less than 22 is [ ]

One less than 20 is [ ]

One less than 16 is 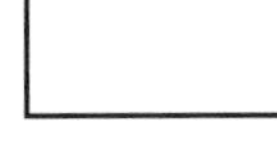

Name ______________________

Five faces

Colour in the faces to match the sums on the right.

     0 + 5 = 5

     1 + 4 = 5

     2 + 3 = 5

     3 + 2 = 5

     4 + 1 = 5

     5 + 0 = 5

Name ___________________________________

Six sailors

6 = ☐ + 6

6 = ☐ + 5

6 = ☐ + 4

6 = ☐ + 3

6 = ☐ + 2

6 = ☐ + 1

6 = ☐ + 0

Name ______________________

Ten tumblers

10 = ☐ + 0

10 = ☐ + 1

10 = ☐ + 2

10 = ☐ + 3

10 = ☐ + 4

10 = ☐ + 5

10 = ☐ + 6

10 = ☐ + 7

10 = ☐ + 8

10 = ☐ + 9

10 = ☐ + 10

SCHOLASTIC
www.scholastic.co.uk

Name ______________________________

Sorting sheep

- How many sheep are in each field? Write your answers in the boxes.
- Then draw a line connecting the boxes, starting with the largest flock and finishing with the smallest.

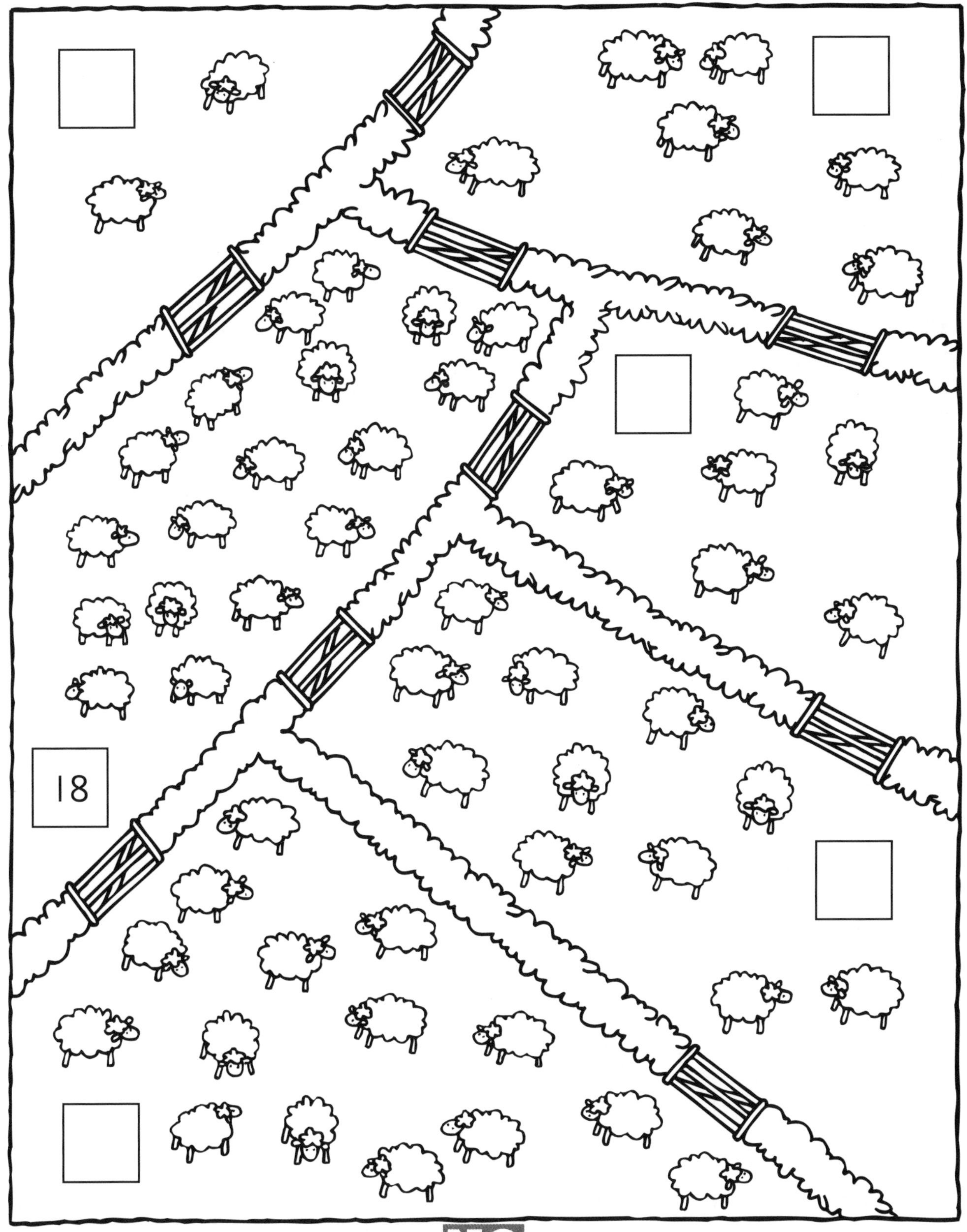

Name ____________________

Three jumps to 6

- How can you get to **6** in three jumps?

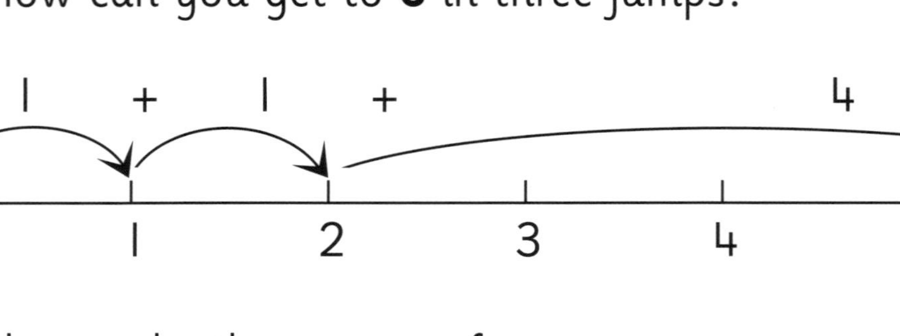

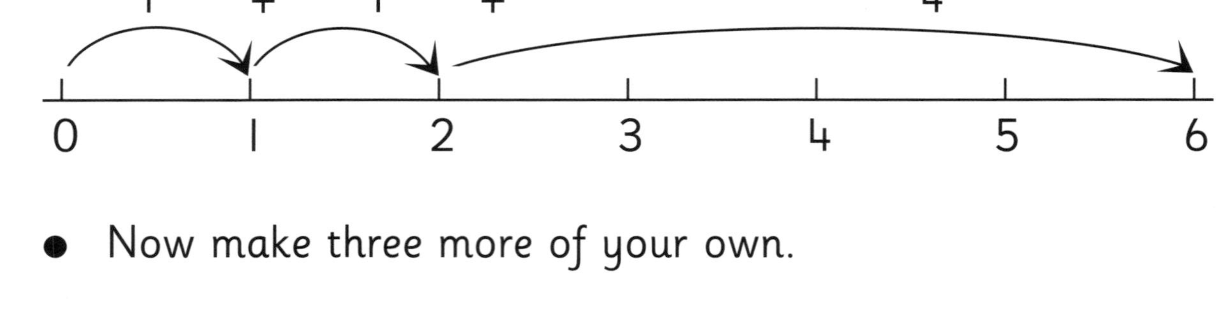

1 + 1 + 4 = 6

- Now make three more of your own.

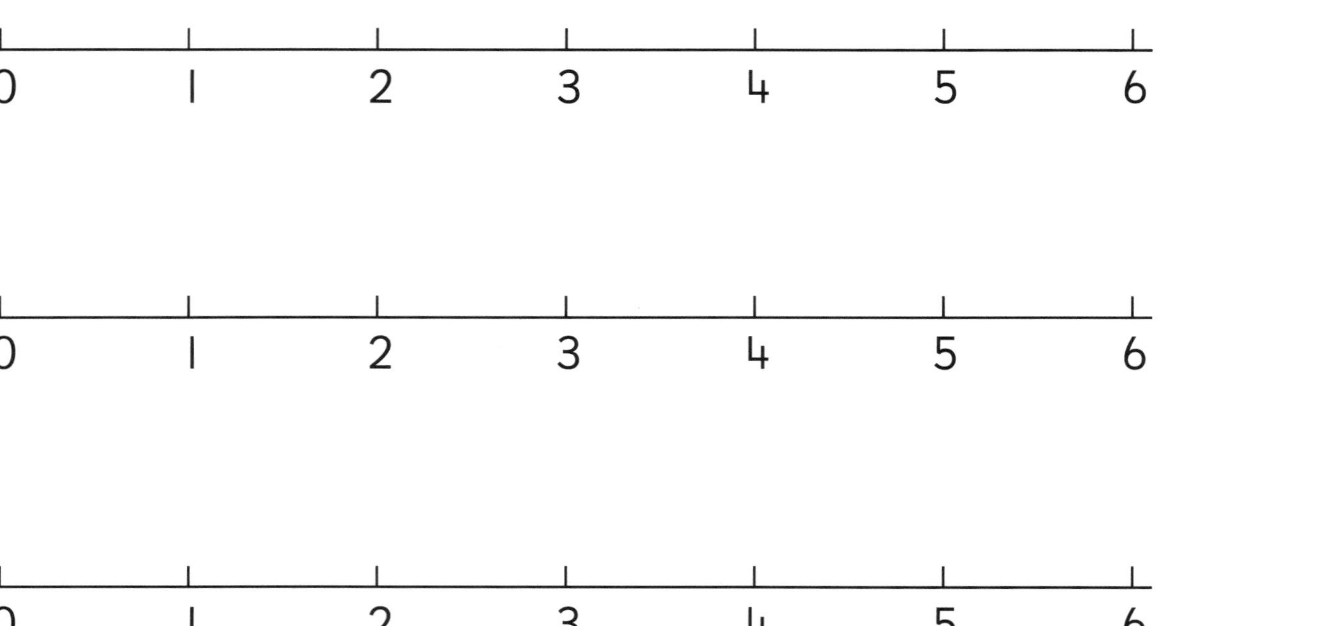

Name ____________________

Three jumps to 10

- How can you get to **10** in three jumps?

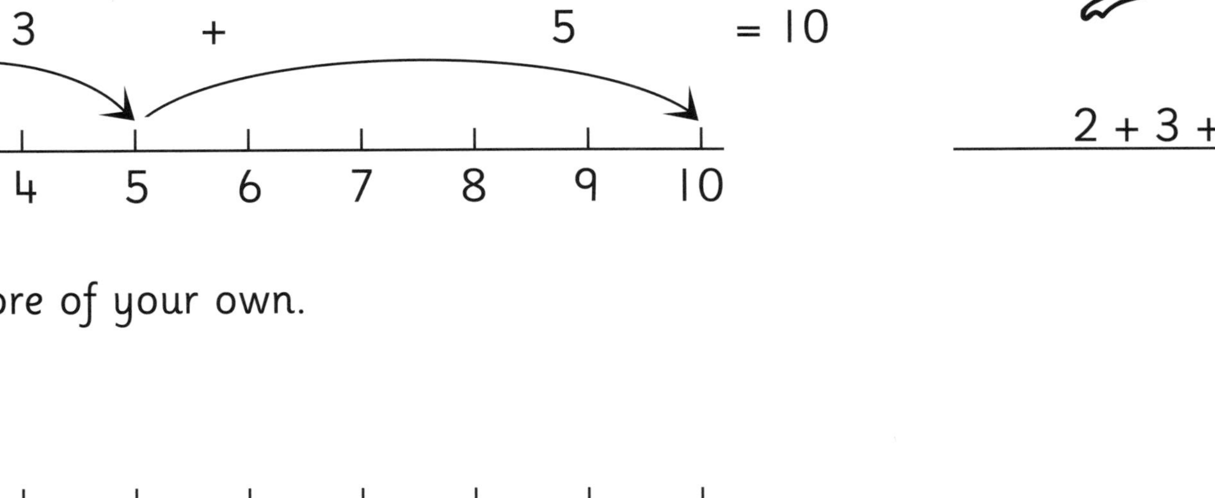

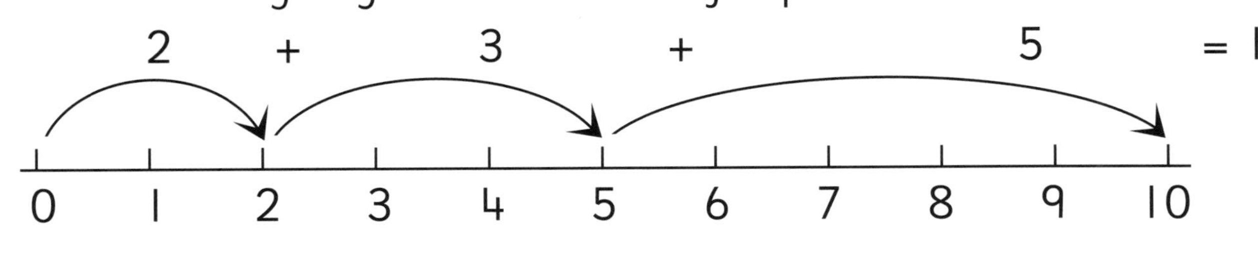

2 + 3 + 5 = 10

- Now make three more of your own.

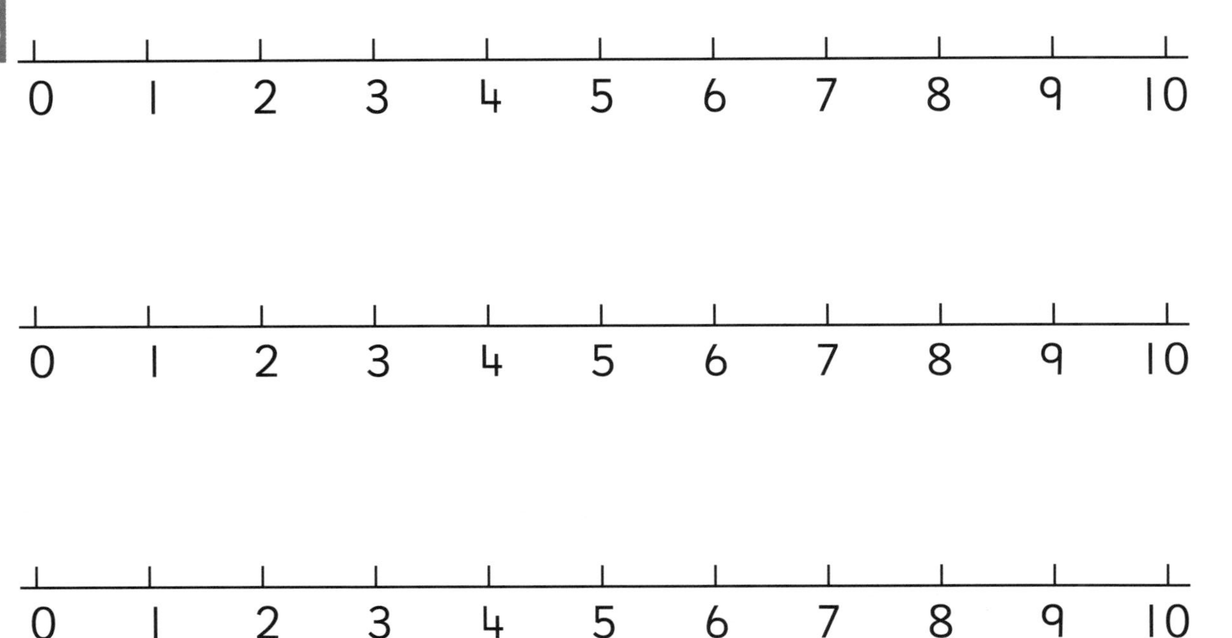

Name ______________________

Blank arithmetic

Use the number line to help you fill in the blanks.

0 1 2 3 4 5 6 7 8 9 10 11 12 13 14 15 16 17 18 19 20 21 22 23 24 25

3 + 3 = ☐	12 + 3 = ☐	17 + 6 = ☐
1 + 8 = ☐	16 + 4 = ☐	14 + 8 = ☐
5 + 6 = ☐	12 + 5 = ☐	19 + 6 = ☐
	11 + 7 = ☐	

SCHOLASTIC
www.scholastic.co.uk

Name ______________________

More blank arithmetic

- Look at how this sum can be made.

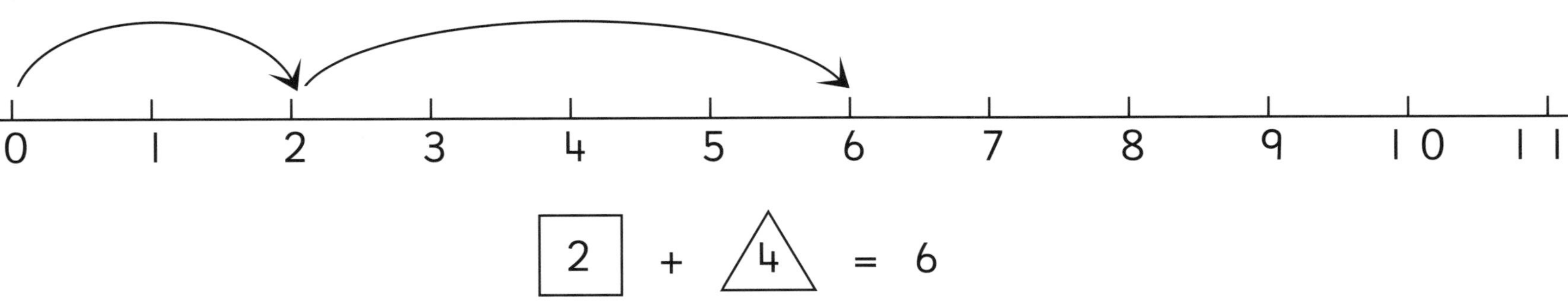

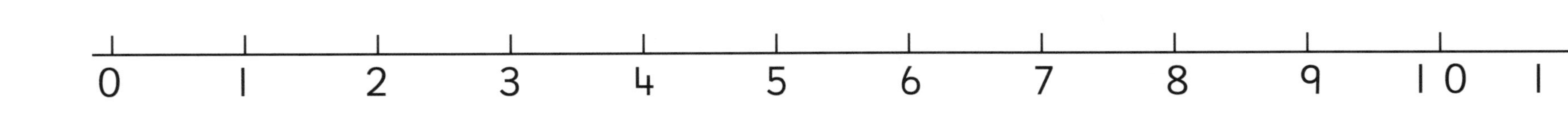

- Now make up your own sums.

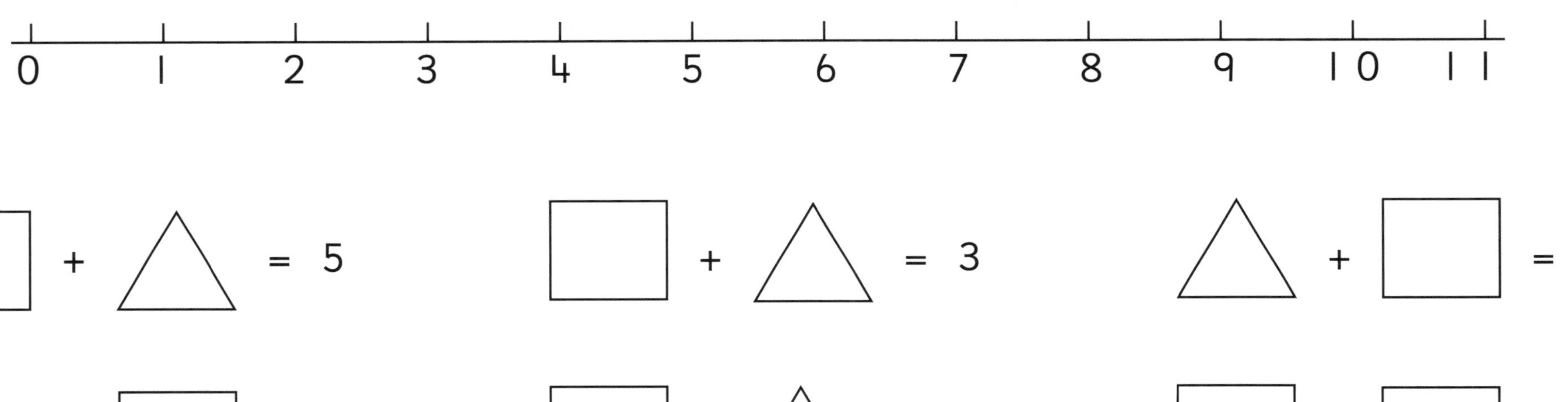

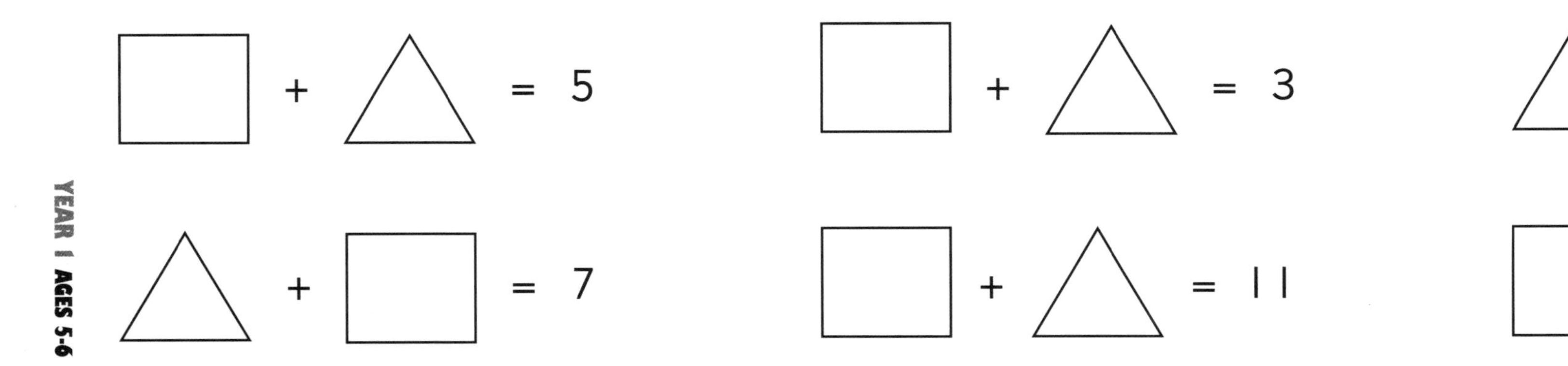

Name ____________________

Spending money

How much did these children spend?

I bought one cornet for 10p.

I bought three cornets for ______ p.

I bought one lolly for 20p.

I bought three lollies for ______ p.

I bought one tub for 15p.

I bought two tubs for ______ p.

Name ____________________

Find the difference

What is the difference between these groups of objects?
Write your answers in the boxes.

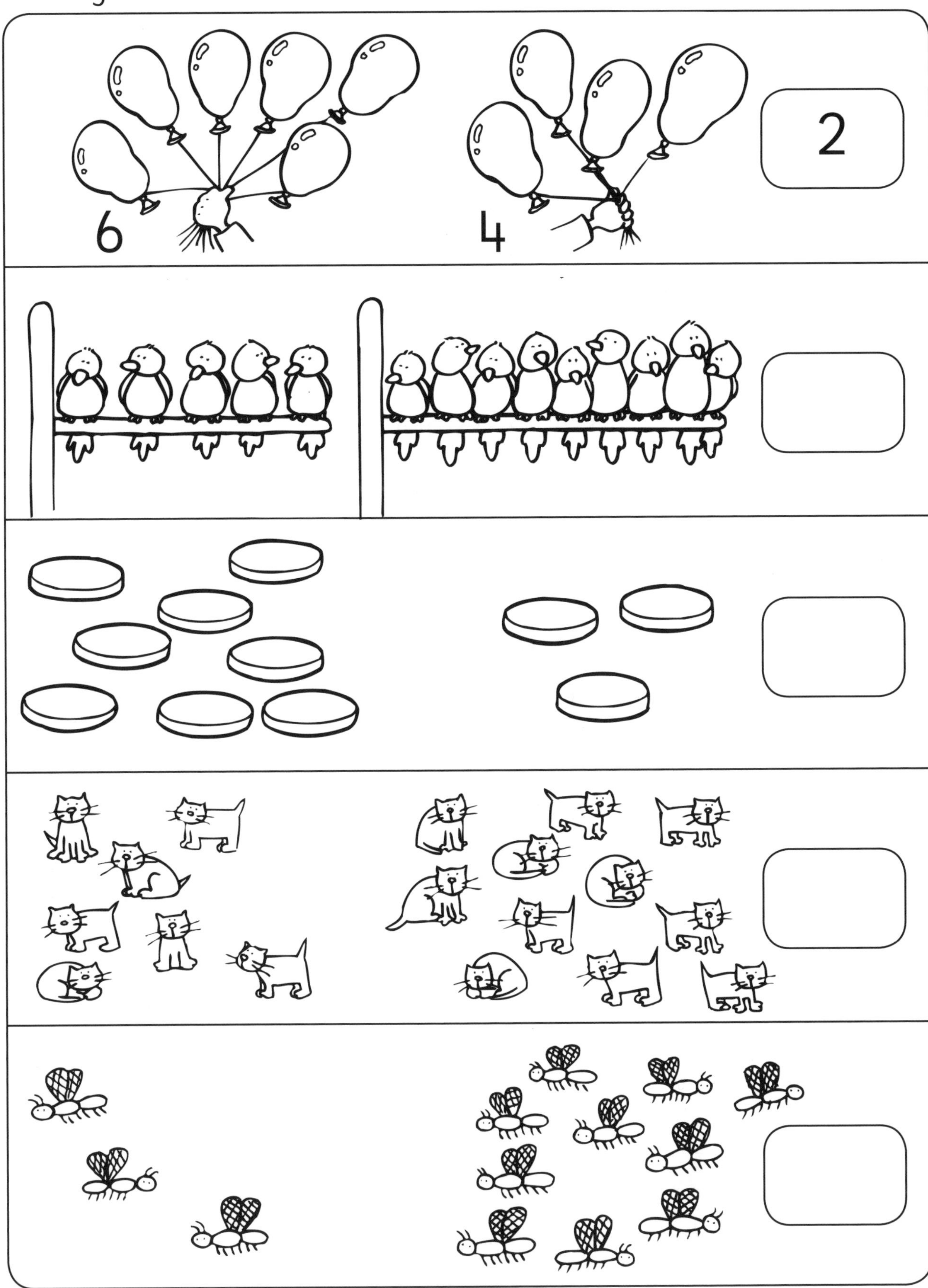

Name ______________________

Guess Nelly's numbers

Nelly takes away 3
Her answer is 7
Nelly's number is:

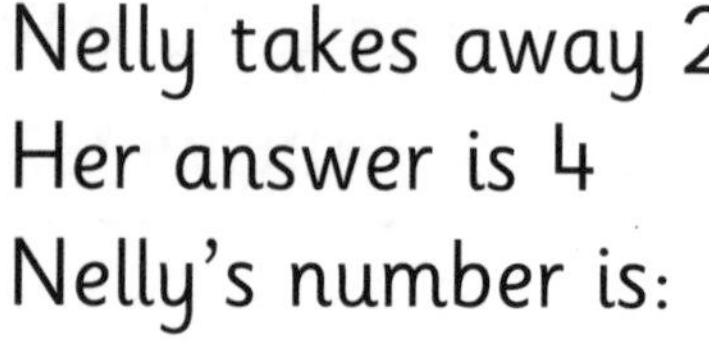

Nelly takes away 2
Her answer is 4
Nelly's number is:

Nelly takes away 4
Her answer is 10
Nelly's number is:

Nelly subtracts 3
Her answer is 5
Nelly's number is:

Nelly subtracts 5
Her answer is 8
Nelly's number is:

SCHOLASTIC
www.scholastic.co.uk

Name ______________________________

Seeing double

toes	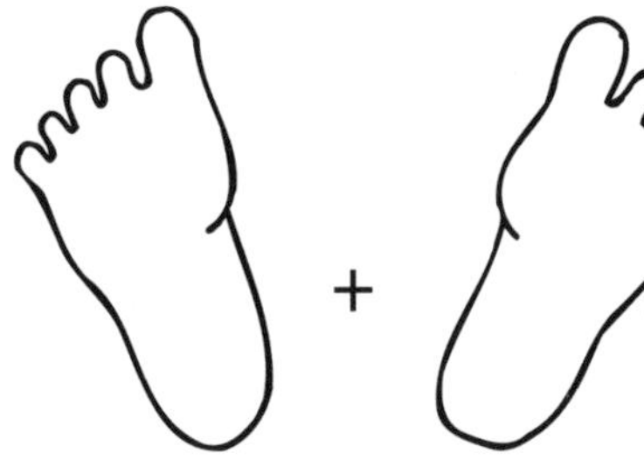		5 + 5 = 10
legs	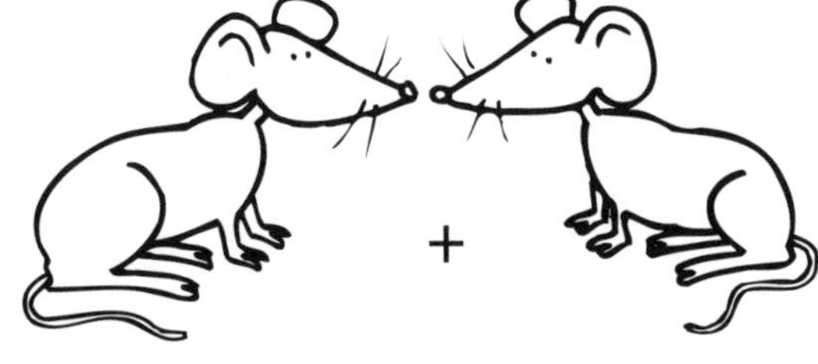		☐ + ☐ = ☐
wheels		+ 	☐ + ☐ = ☐
ears		+ 	☐ + ☐ = ☐
noses		+ 	☐ + ☐ = ☐
spots		+ 	☐ + ☐ = ☐

Name ______________________

Time passing

From 8 o'clock to 9 o'clock is ______ hour.

From 9 o'clock to 12 o'clock is ______ hours.

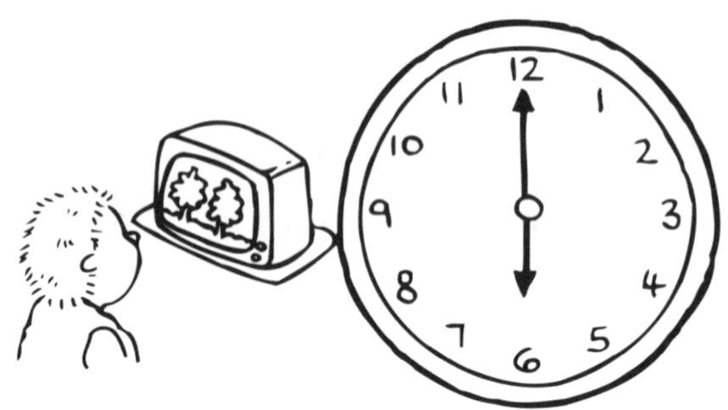

From 3 o'clock to 6 o'clock is ______ hours.

From 4 o'clock to 7 o'clock is ______ hours.

SCHOLASTIC
www.scholastic.co.uk

Name ______________________________

Sorting shapes

How many sides and corners does each shape have?
Write your answers in the circles.

◯ long sides ◯ short sides	◯ corners ◯ sides
◯ corners ◯ sides	◯ sides ◯ corners
◯ long sides ◯ short sides	◯ long sides ◯ short sides

Name ____________________

Where am I?

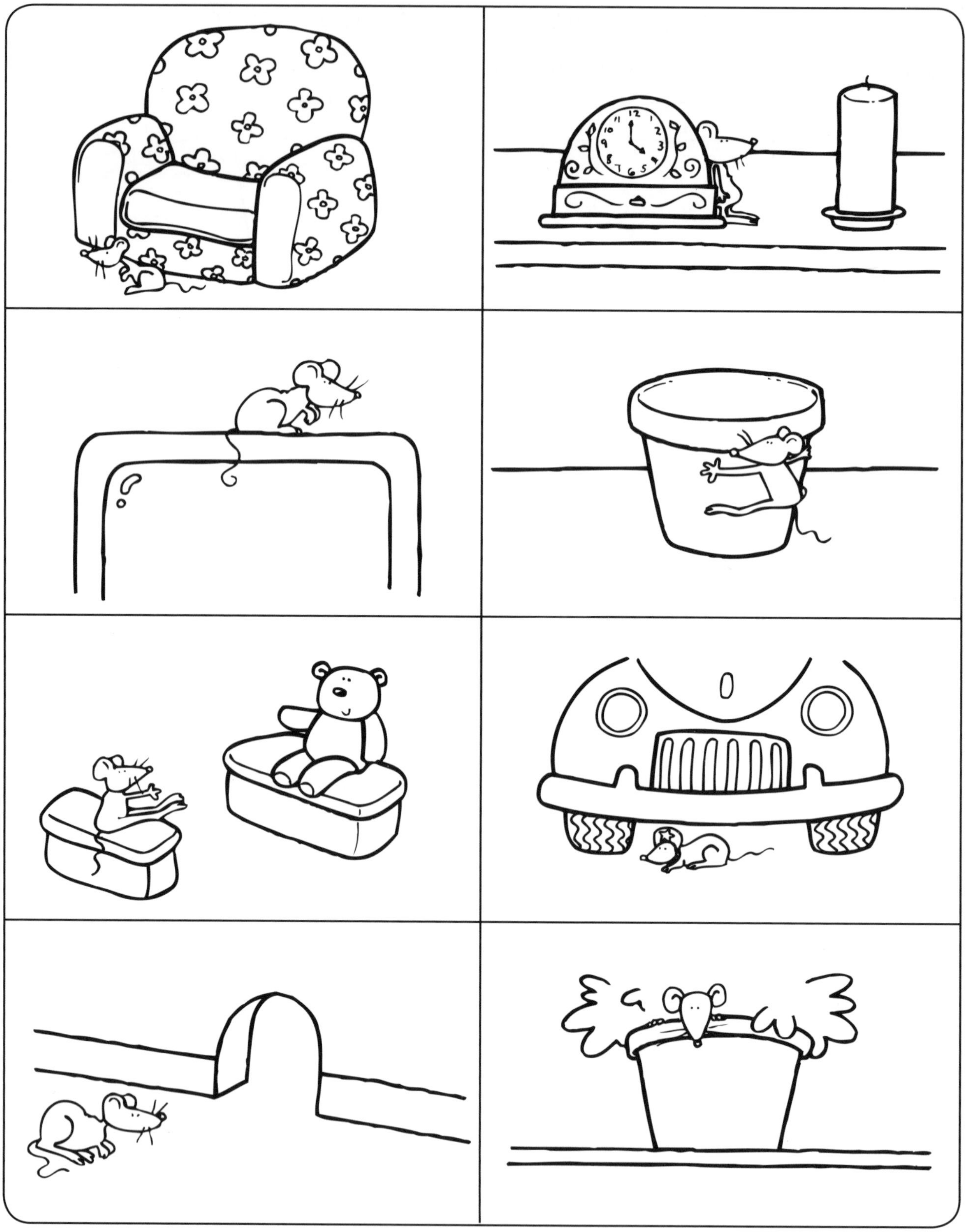

underneath | next to | inside | close to | near | on

above | outside | on top of | opposite | in front of

Name ____________________

Am I an animal?

Sort the pictures into the correct box.

animals	other

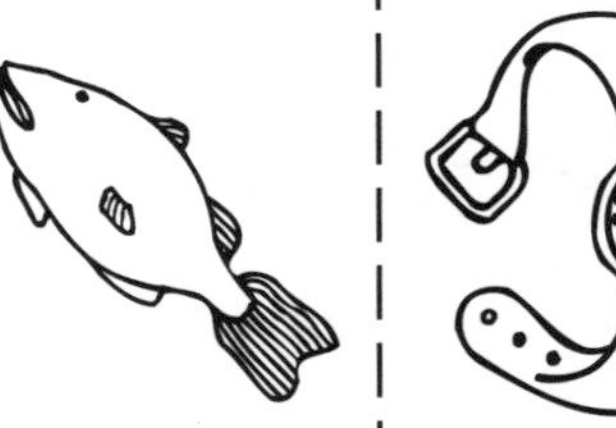

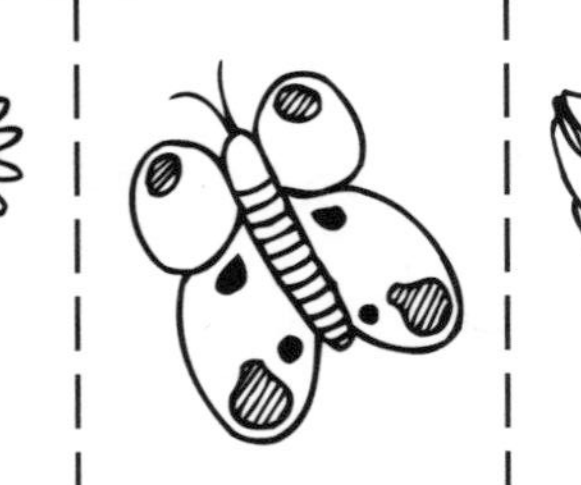

Name ____________________

Adults and young

Match the young animal to the adult.

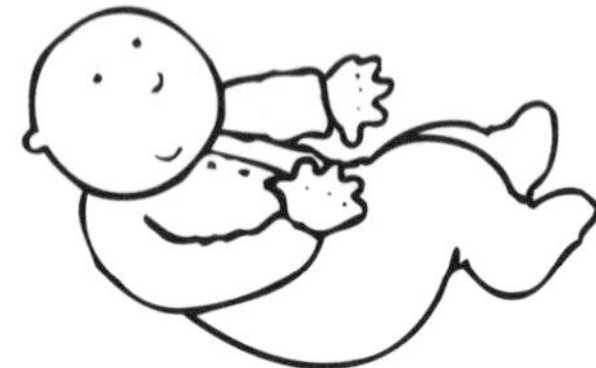

Name ____________________

Alive and not alive

Sort the pictures into the correct box.

Name ________________________________

Growing food

We eat some plants. Which might end up on your plate?
Draw a line from the plants we can eat to the plate.

Name ______________________________

Material mad

Is this sensible? What do you think these clothes **should** be made from? Write your answers in the boxes.

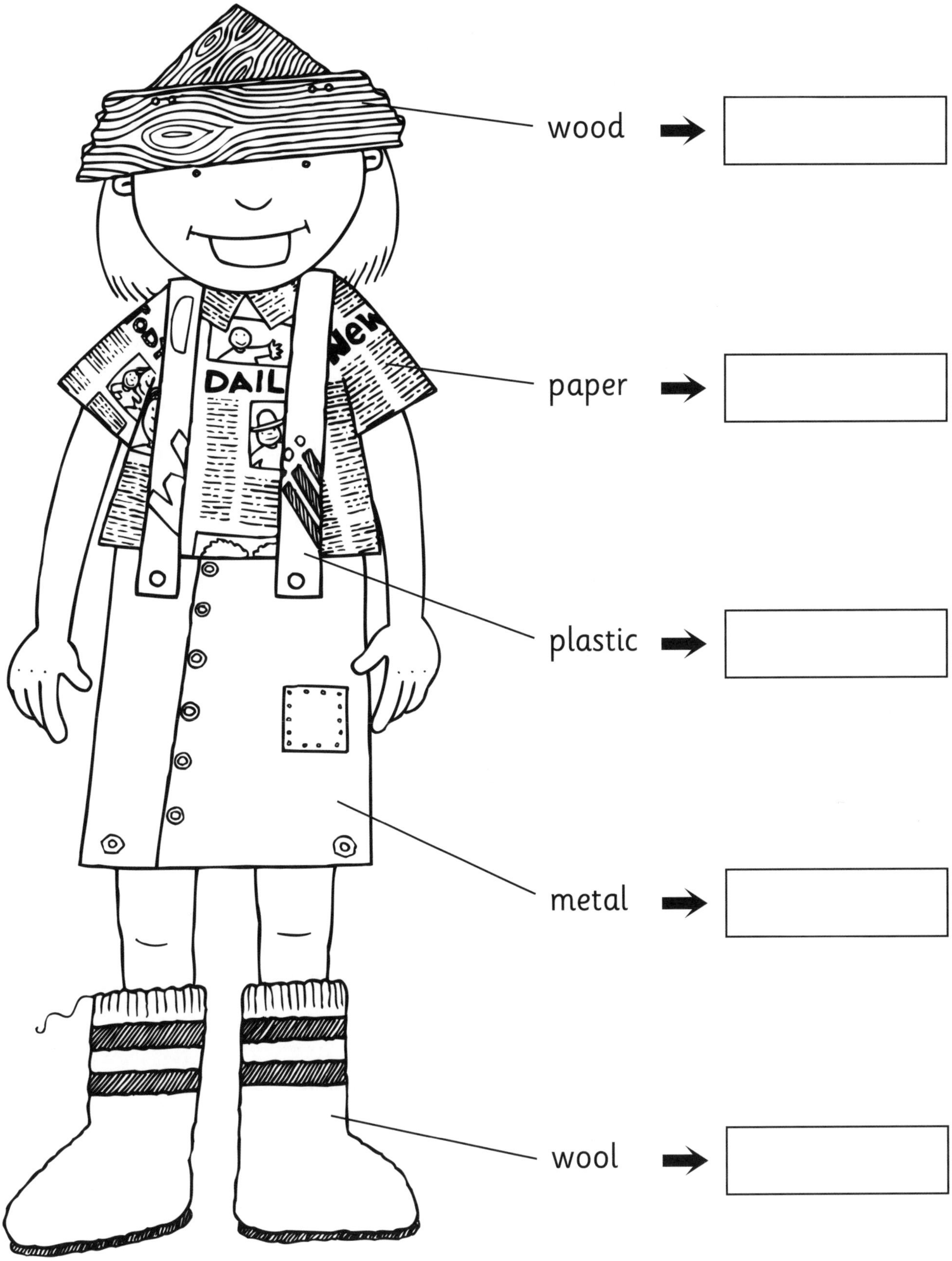

wood ➔ [ ]

paper ➔ [ ]

plastic ➔ [ ]

metal ➔ [ ]

wool ➔ [ ]

Name ______________________

How does it look and feel?

- Write each material in the chart below.
- What words can you think of to describe them?

	describing words
fabric	

Name ______________________

What's it like?

- Choose an object and draw it in the circle.
- Write describing words on the lines.

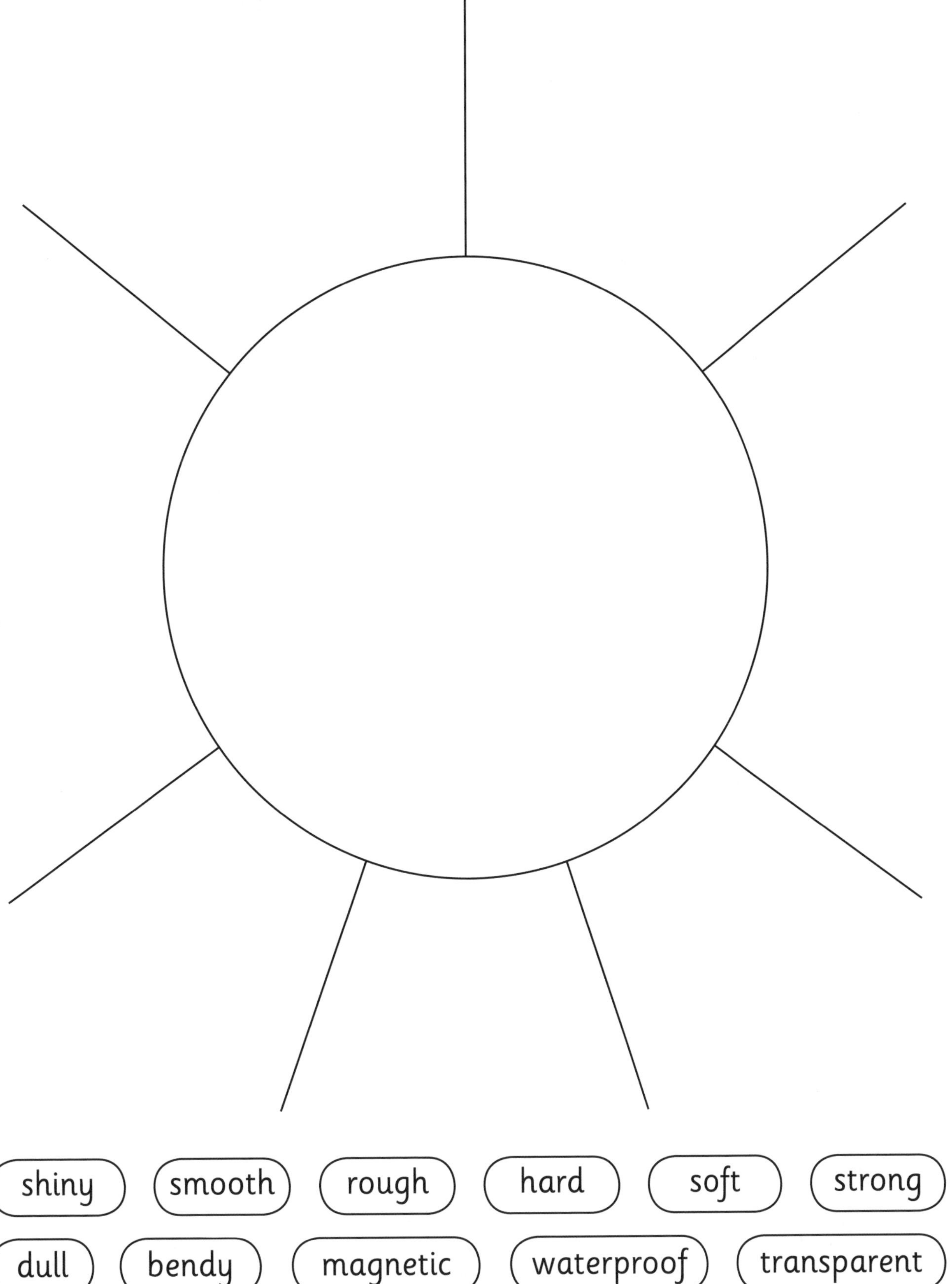

shiny smooth rough hard soft strong

dull bendy magnetic waterproof transparent

Name ____________________

What could you use to...?

Write down materials that you could use...

	to wrap a parcel ____________________
	to make a shirt ____________________
	to hold a drink ____________________
	to build a hutch ____________________
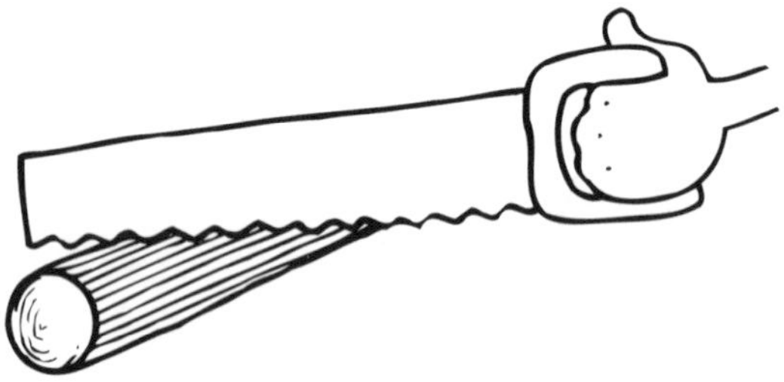	to make a saw ____________________

Materials: plastic, glass, string, cotton, metal, wood, paper, clay, fabric

SCHOLASTIC
www.scholastic.co.uk

Name ______________________________

Light and dark

- Use colours to show where the light comes from at night.

- Where does the light come from in the daytime?

Name ______________________

Ways to move

How are these children moving?

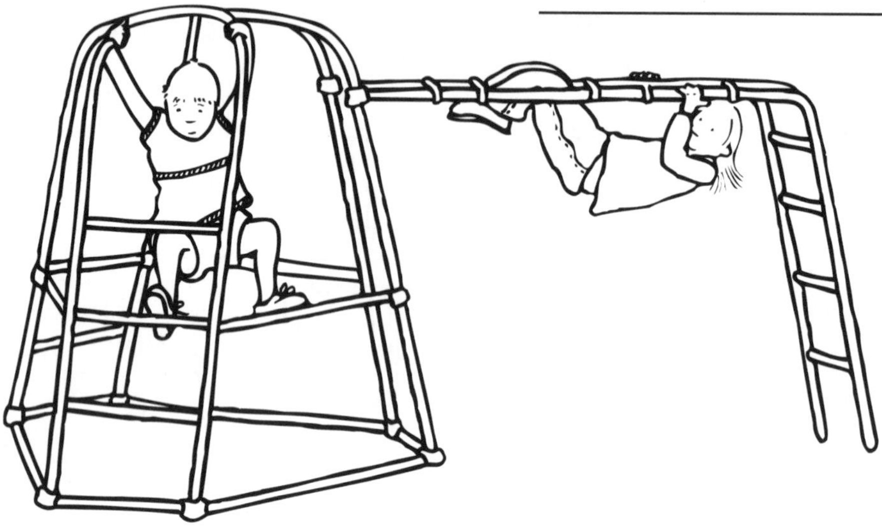

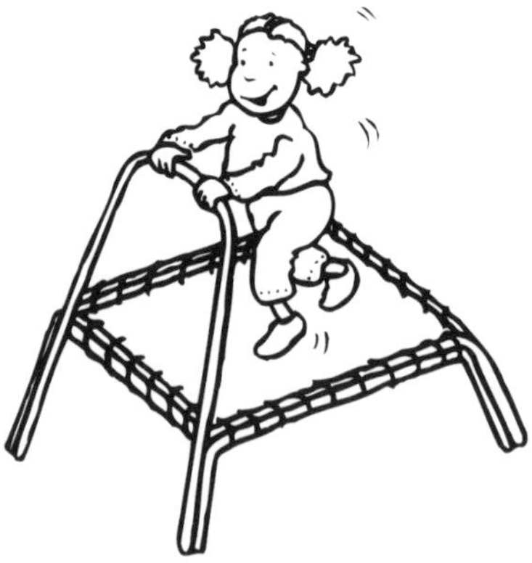

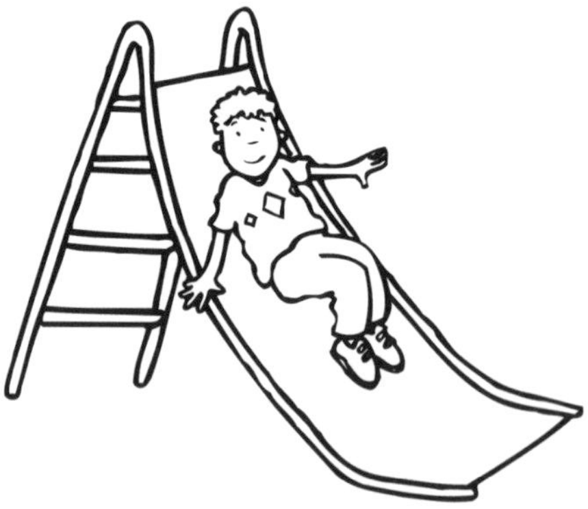

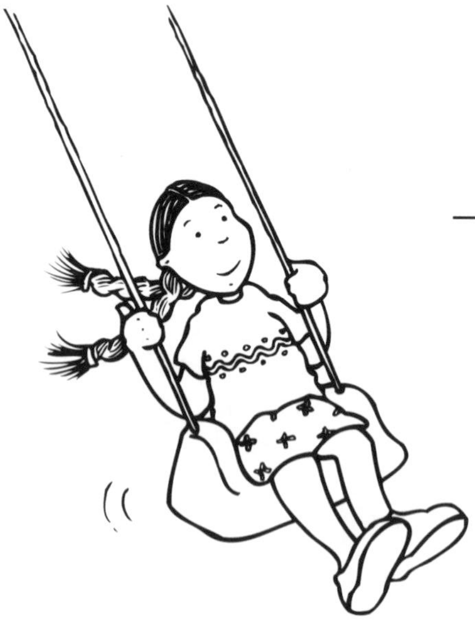

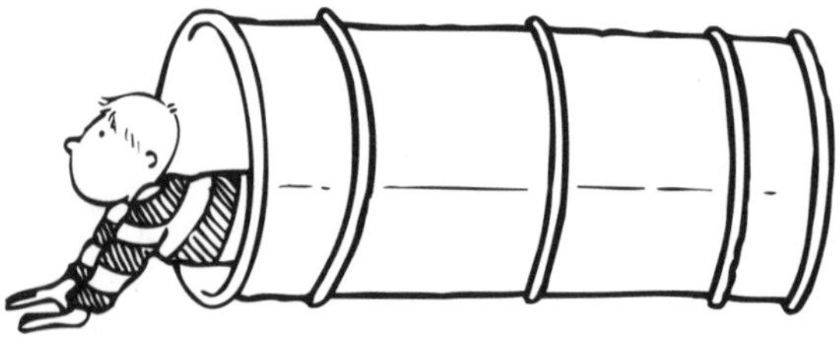

____

____

____

____

____

____

jumping | swinging | sliding

crawling | climbing | twisting

Name ____________________

Push and pull

Write **push** or **pull** in the arrows.

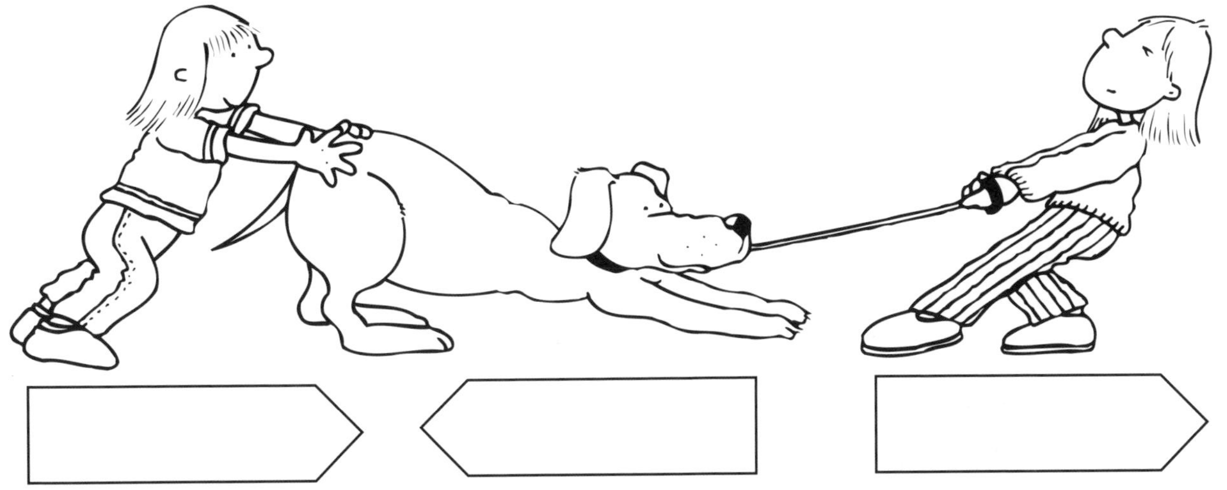

Name ____________________________

Pushing and pulling at home

When do you push and pull at home?
Write the correct word in the spaces.

pulling pushing

I shut the door by ____________________.

I open the door by ____________________.

I shut the drawer by ____________________.

I open the drawer by ____________________.

I switch on the light by ____________________.

I open the window by ____________________.

Name ______________________

What makes it move?

Write the correct word in the spaces.

wind water

The ________________

makes the branches move.

The ________________

makes the wheel turn.

The 

makes the sailing boat move.

The ________________

makes the washing move.

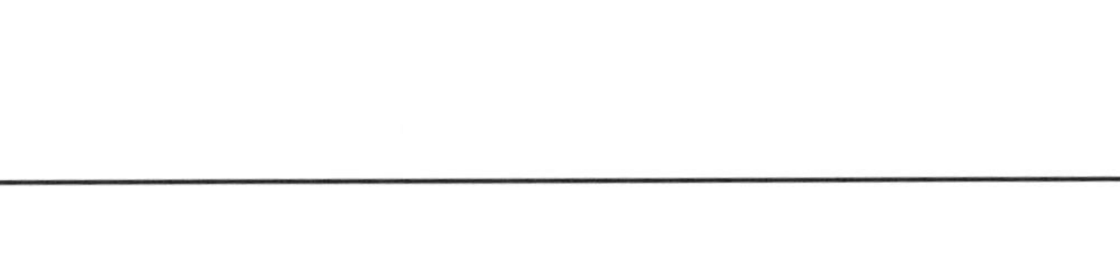

Name ______________________

Watch out! Because...

Stick labels on the dangers in this picture. Say why.

Be careful!

Be careful!

Be careful!

Be careful!

Be careful!

Name ______________________________

Barmy band

- What's wrong with this band?

- Choose the correct word from the box to complete the sentences. We should...

______________________ a triangle.

______________________ a drum.

______________________ a trumpet.

______________________ a tambourine.

______________________ a guitar.

pluck
hit
shake
bang
blow

Name ______________________________

Loud or quiet?

- Describe the sounds.

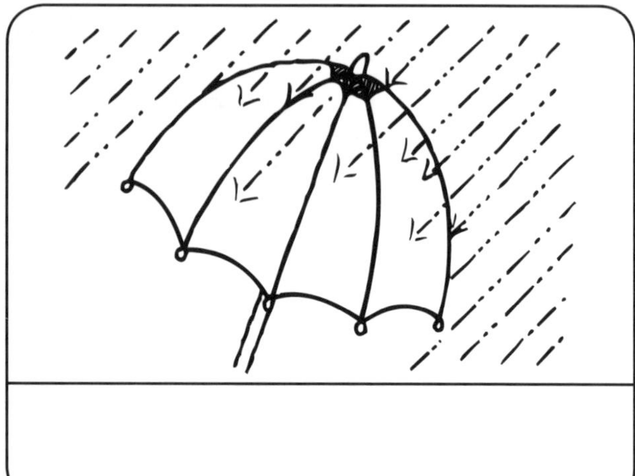

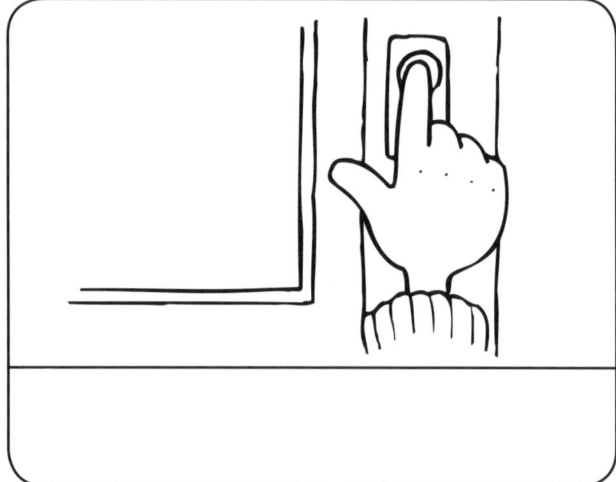

loud | soft | quiet | high | low

- Can you think of any more words?

Name ______________________________

Sounds I can make

What sounds are these children making?

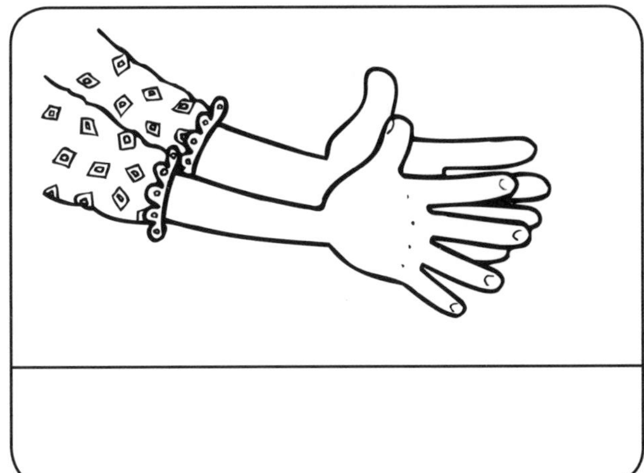

crying	stamping	singing
clapping	whistling	whispering

Name ______________________

Old and new

Describe these toys.

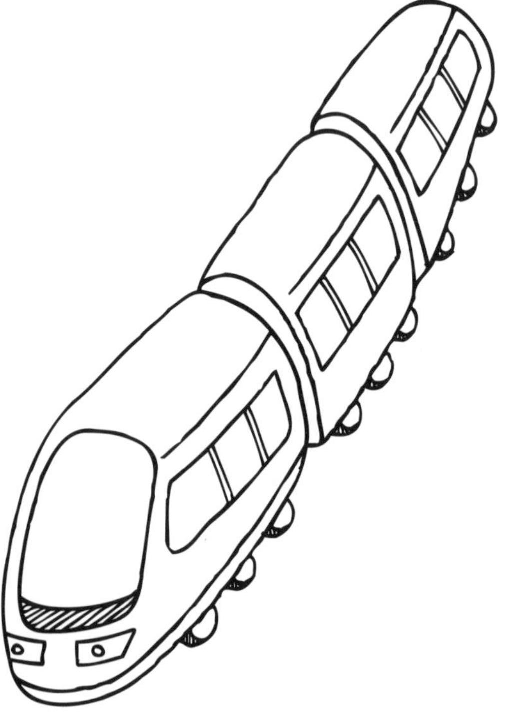

clean	shiny	metal	plastic	worn	
dirty	broken	modern	old	used	new

Name ______________________________

Where people live

- Which home is most like yours?
- Draw your home in the blank square.

My home

Name ______________________

A house from the past

- Match the words to the correct part of the house.
- How is this house different from your home?

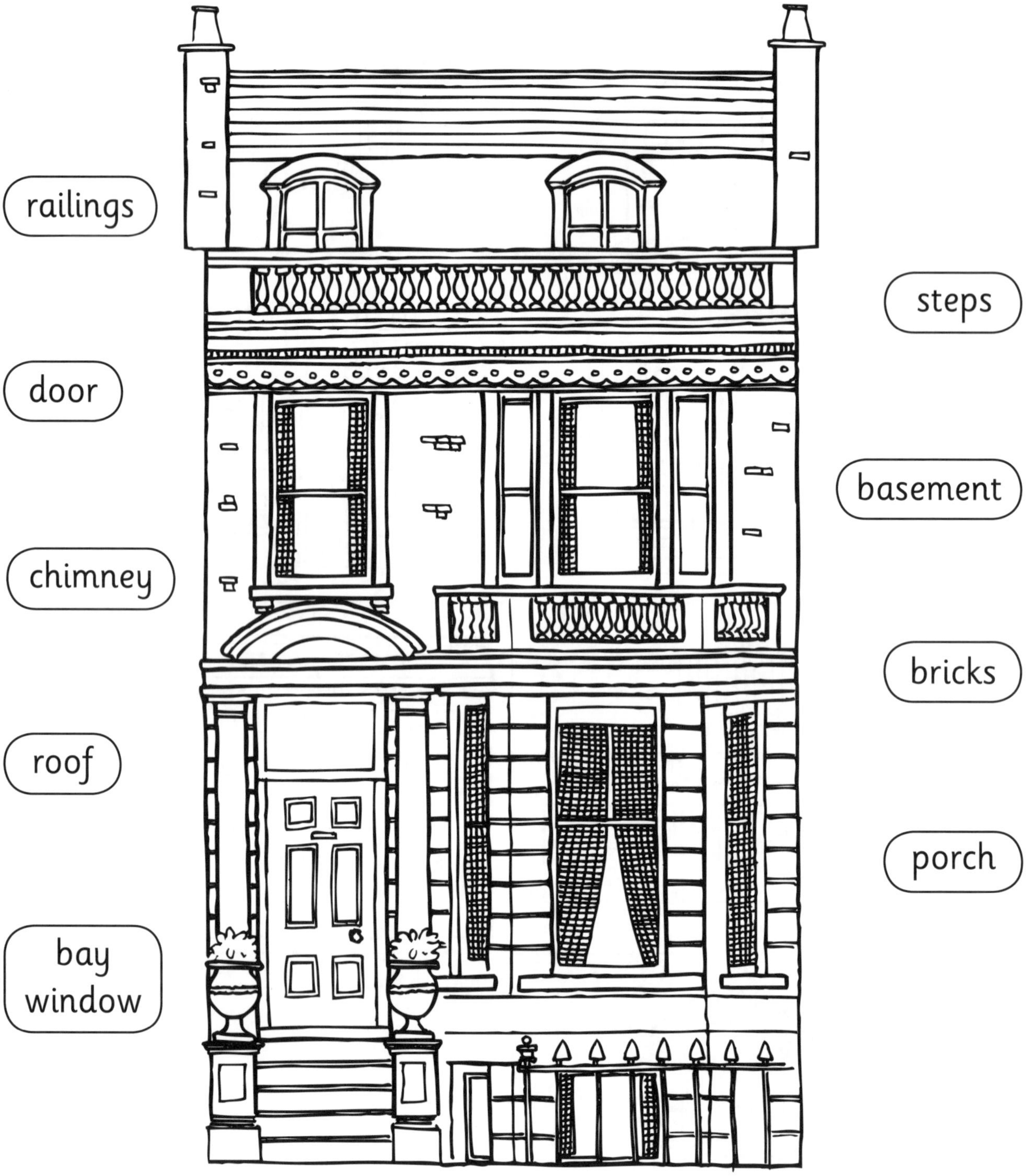

railings

door

chimney

roof

bay window

steps

basement

bricks

porch

SCHOLASTIC
www.scholastic.co.uk

Name ______________________________

Household objects from a long time ago

- What are these objects?
- What were they used for?

____

used for ______________________________

____

used for ______________________________

____

used for ______________________________

____

used for ______________________________

____

used for ______________________________

Bowl and jug | Coal scuttle

Egg whisk | Flat iron | Warming-pan

Name ______________________

Home life

- Describe these objects.
- What are they called?

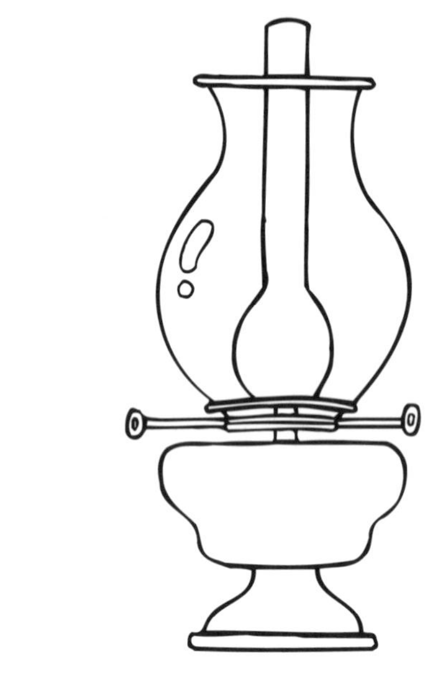

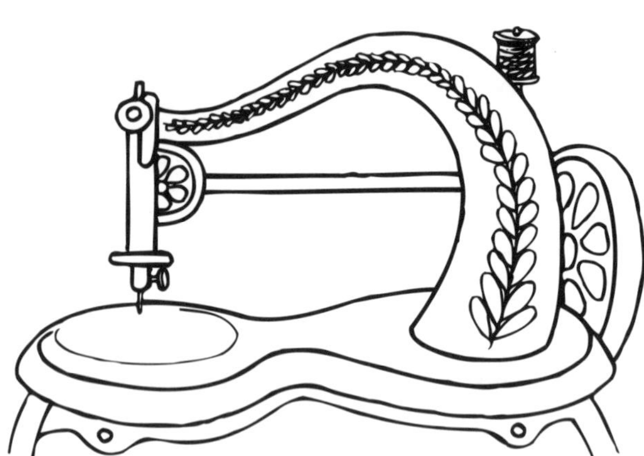

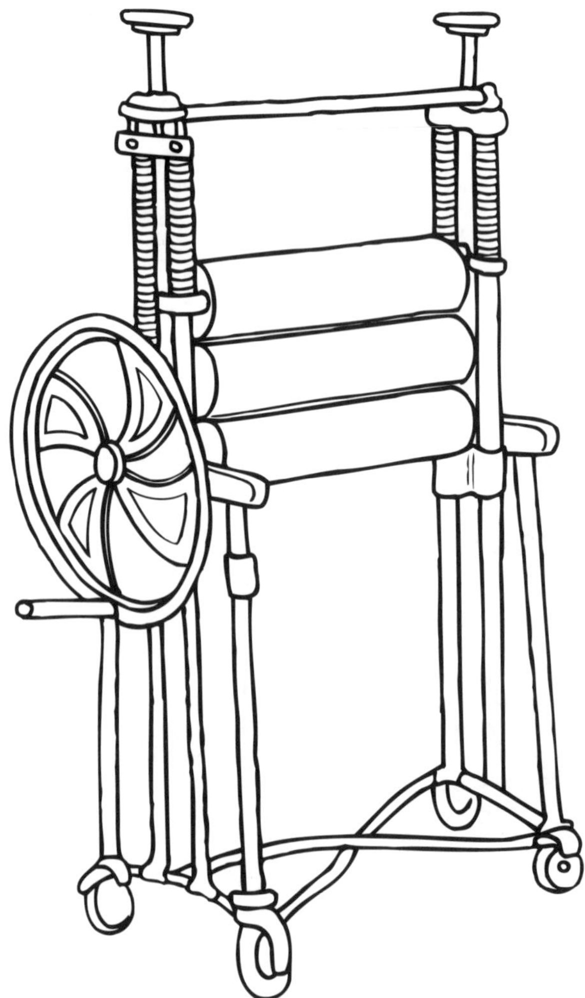

mangle | sewing machine | piano | paraffin lamp

SCHOLASTIC www.scholastic.co.uk

Name ____________________

What has changed?

- Which bus would these people travel on?
- Talk about the changes you can see.

Name ____________________

Going to school

- Ask six friends how they travel to school.
- Cut out stickers for them and stick them in the right column.

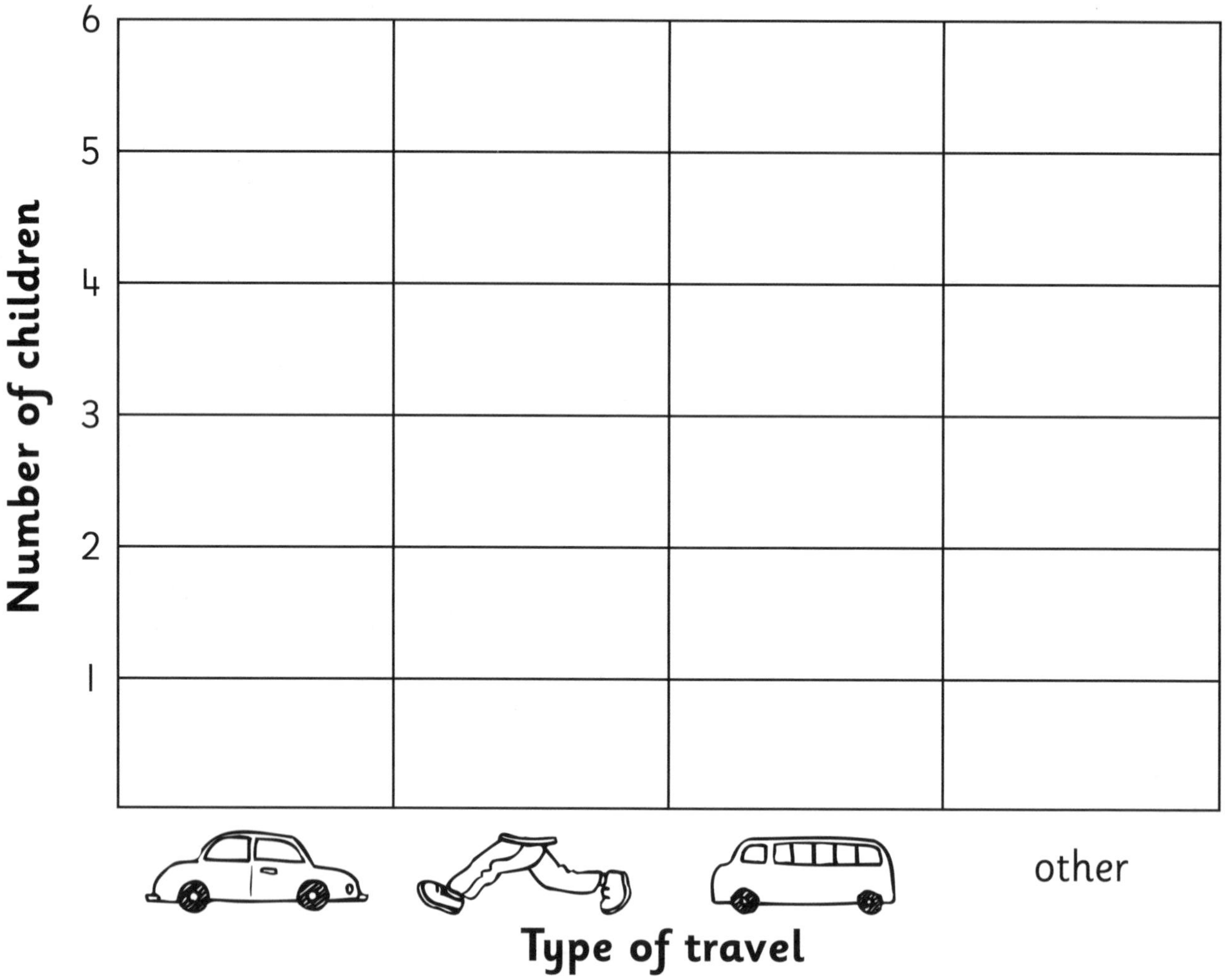

Number of children

6				
5				
4				
3				
2				
1				
				other

Type of travel

Travel stickers

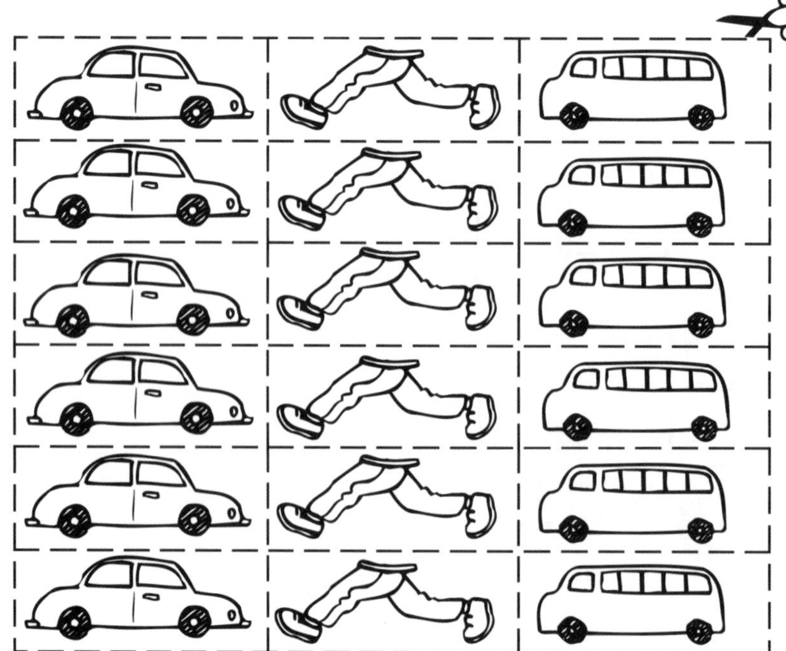

Name ______________________________

On the way to school

- Fill in the missing pictures.
- Then tick what you pass on the way to school.

Name ______________________

Where I live

Who lives where? Match the characters to their addresses.

Miss B. Peep
14 Sheep Close
Crook
Durham
DU7 6RN

Miss R. R. Hood
1 Forest Road
Wolverhampton
WV4 6RN

Miss L. Muffett
32 Tuffet Street
Weybridge
GU7 2BB

Mr H. Dumpty
5 Brick Drive
Wallsend
NE4 3GG

Name ______________________________

Nice and nasty

- Colour the places that you think are nice. Why are they nice?

- Draw a nice part of your town. Why is it nice?

Name ______________________________

Leisure tally

- Ask some adults about their favourite leisure activities. Put a mark (I) for each person's favourite.
- Which is the most popular? Colour the activities that need a special building.

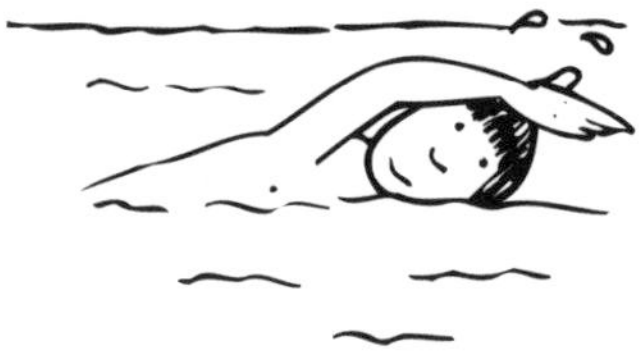

				Total

SCHOLASTIC www.scholastic.co.uk

Name ______________________

Making safe

- Choose four things from below that might make your street safe and more pleasant to live in. Can you say why?
- Cut them out and stick them in this space.

Name ____________________

Traffic count

Stand in a safe place with an adult. Colour one space for each vehicle you see.

	1	2	3	4	5	6	7	8	9	10	11	12	13	14	15
other															

Name ______________________________

Moving Ted

Can you find a way of making Ted's arms or legs move?
The objects in the toolbox may help you.

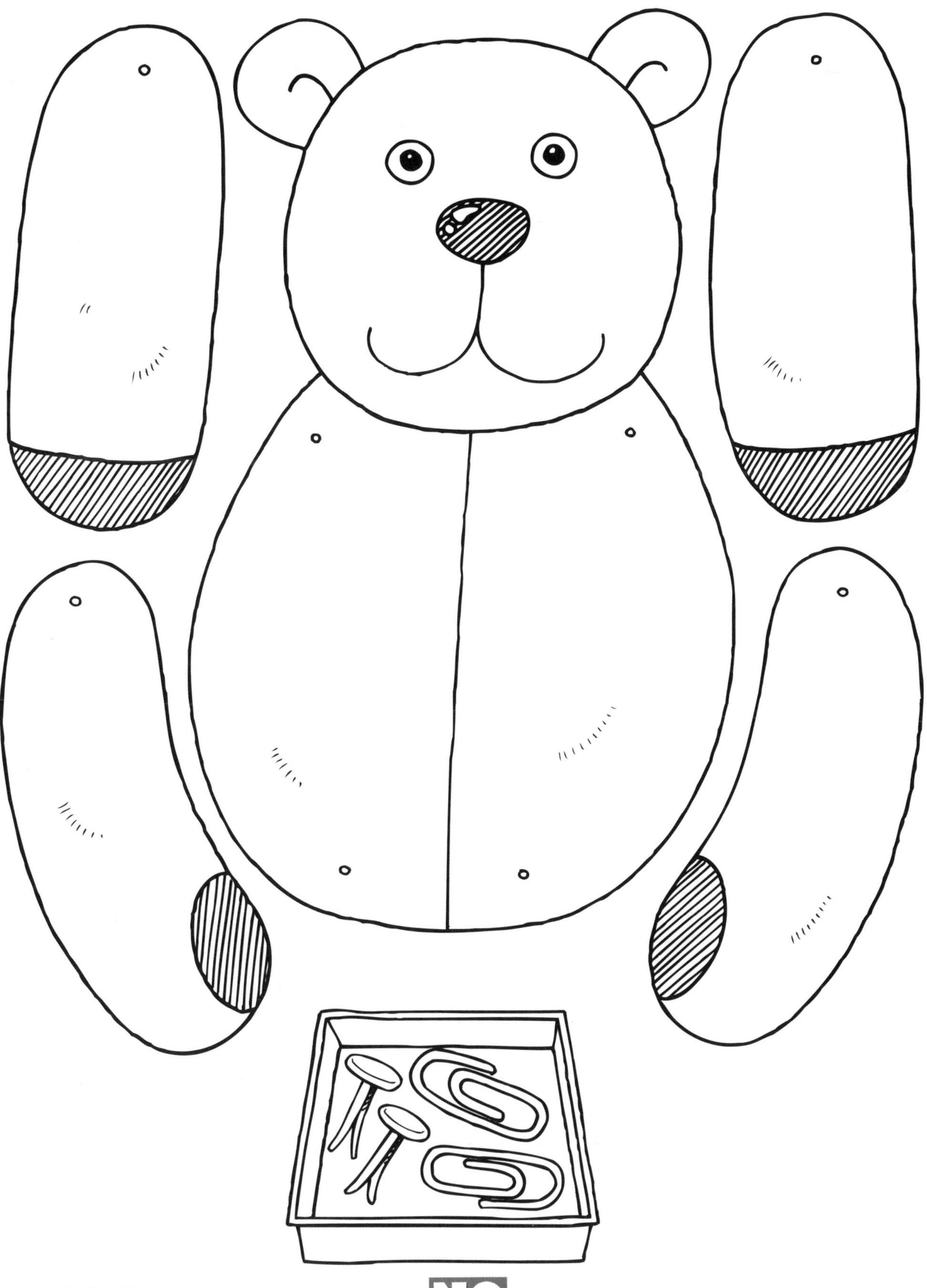

Name ________________

See-saw

- Can you make the see-saw move up and down? Where does the see-saw **pivot**?
- What might you use from the toolbox?

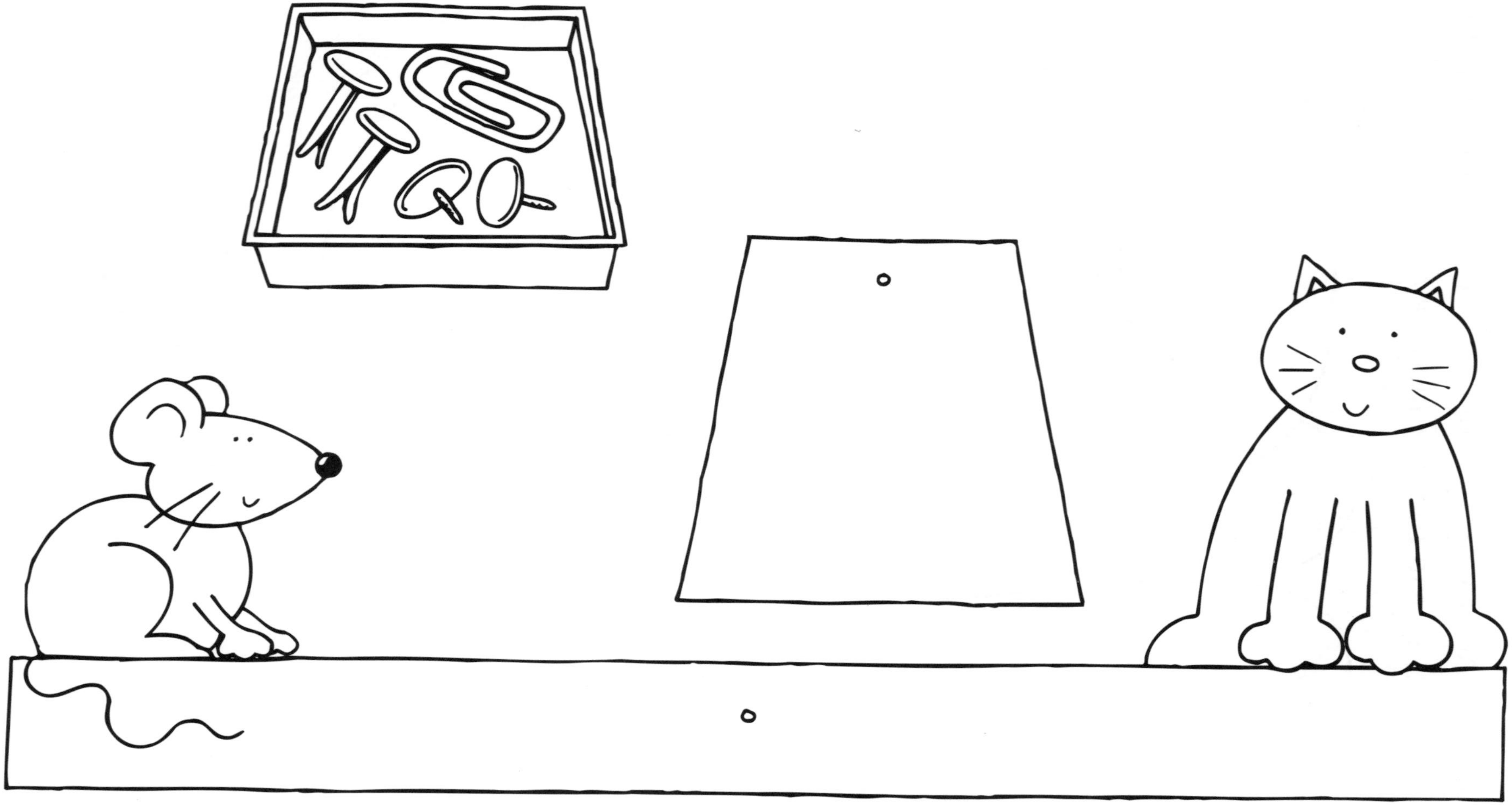

Name ____________________

Fruit and vegetables

- What are the fruit and vegetables below called?

- Which do we **wash** before eating? W

- Which do we **peel** before eating? P

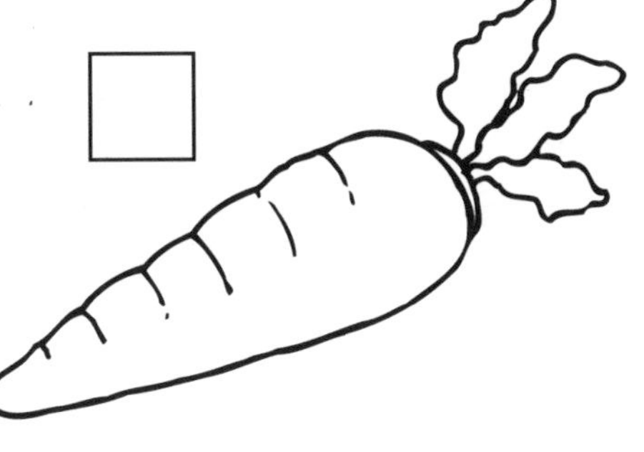

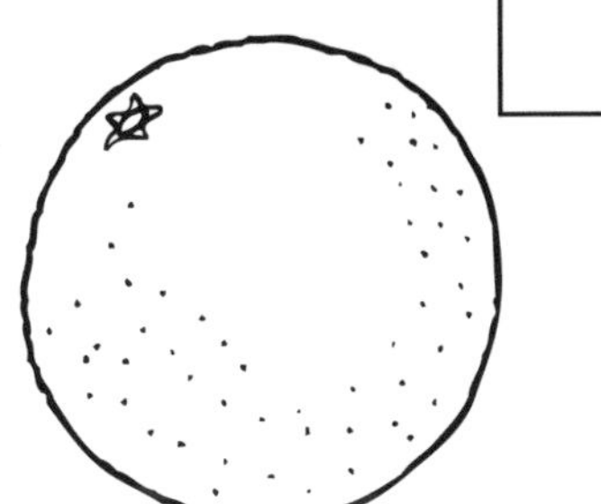
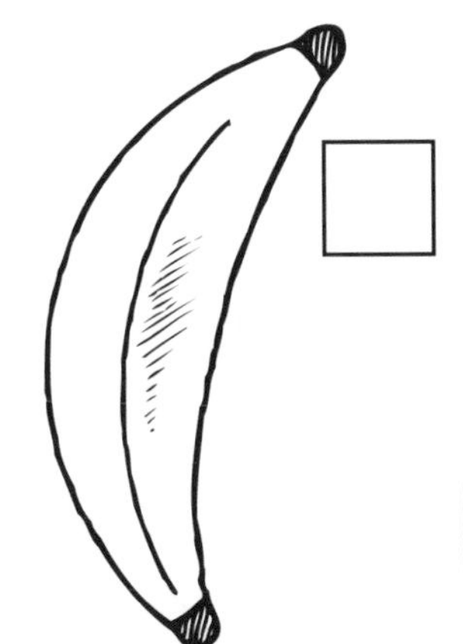

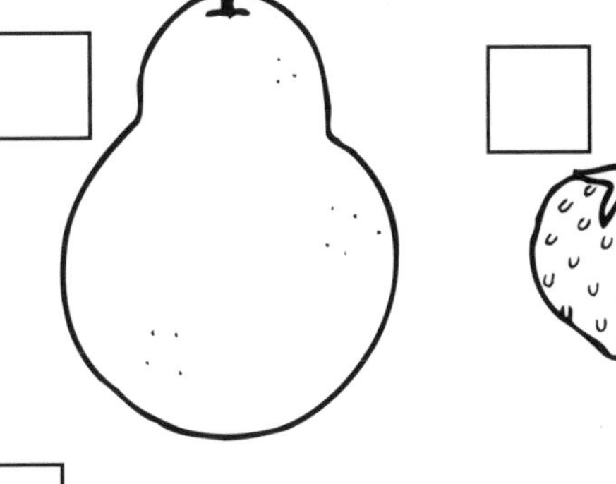
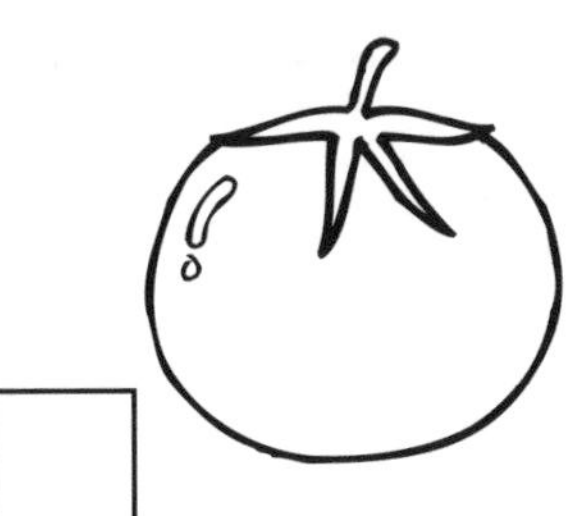
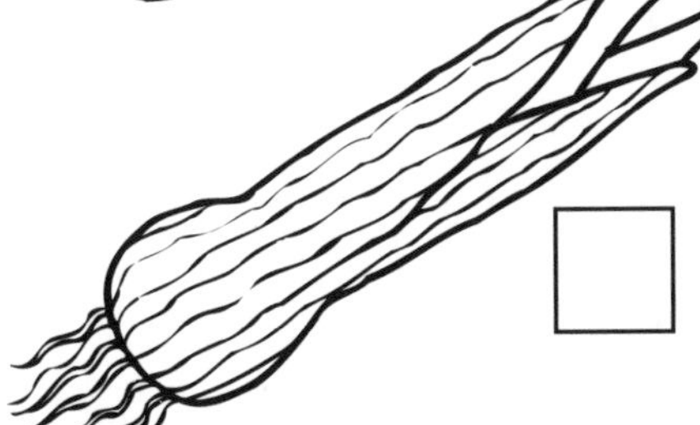

carrot	banana	tomato	apple	strawberry
leek	orange	potato	pear	cauliflower

Name ______________________

Houses can be different

Think of words to describe these houses. What are they made from? Why are they different?

igloo | stilts | tent | brick

detached | snow | sand | water

Name ______________________________

Playtime

- Tick the ones you can find in your playground. What are they called? Find out what they are made from. How have the parts been joined together?

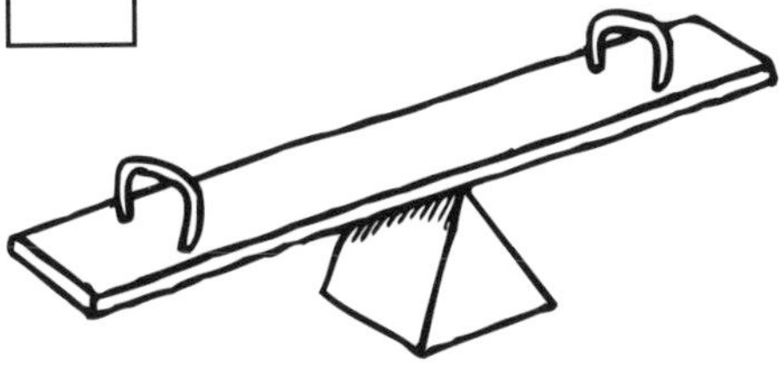

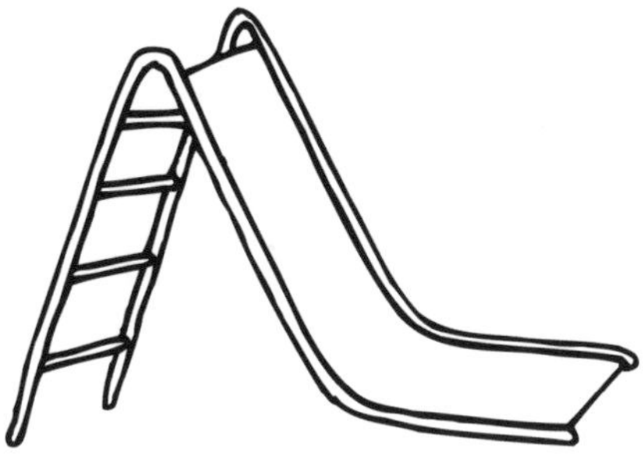

☐ ☐ ☐ ☐ ☐ ☐ ☐

- Design and build a model swing. What will you use?

construction kit | cardboard | egg box | string

Name ______________________

Reading pictures

- What do these pictures tell us?

______________________ ______________________

______________________ ______________________

no swimming | toilets | bumpy road | telephone

- What do these computer icons tell us?

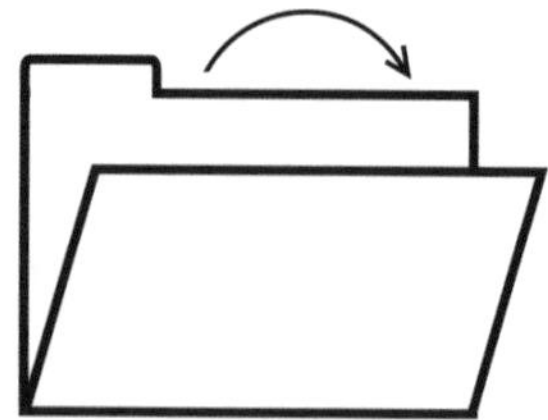
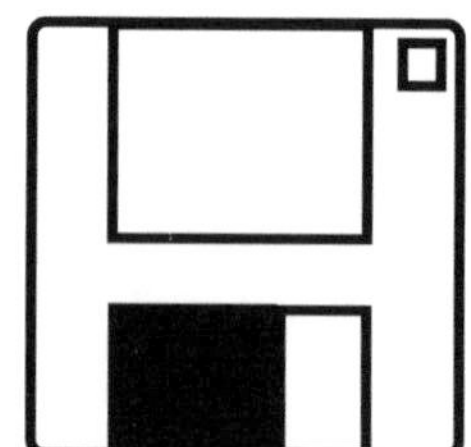

__________ __________ __________ __________

cut | print | save | open

Name ____________________

Icon chart

- Look at the computer screen and make a chart of some **icons**.
- Write what they mean.

Icon	means
	print

Name ______________________________

Sorting animals

Put the animals in the correct sets.

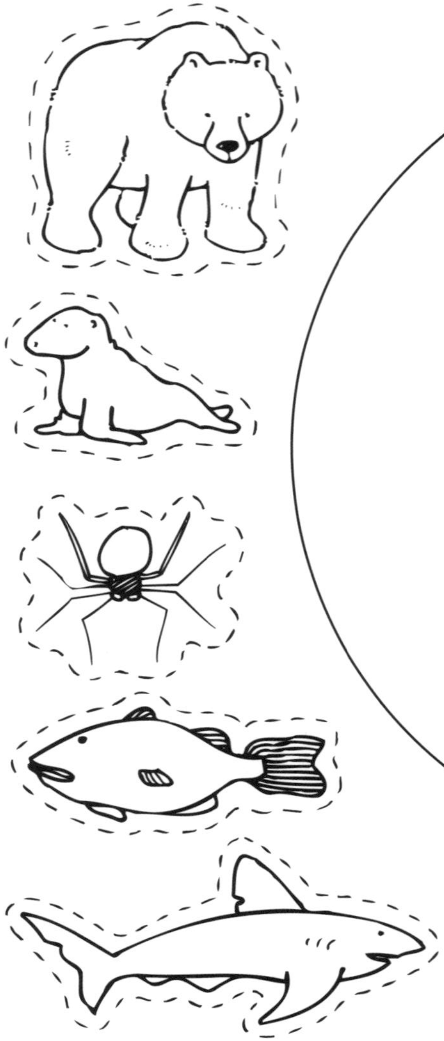

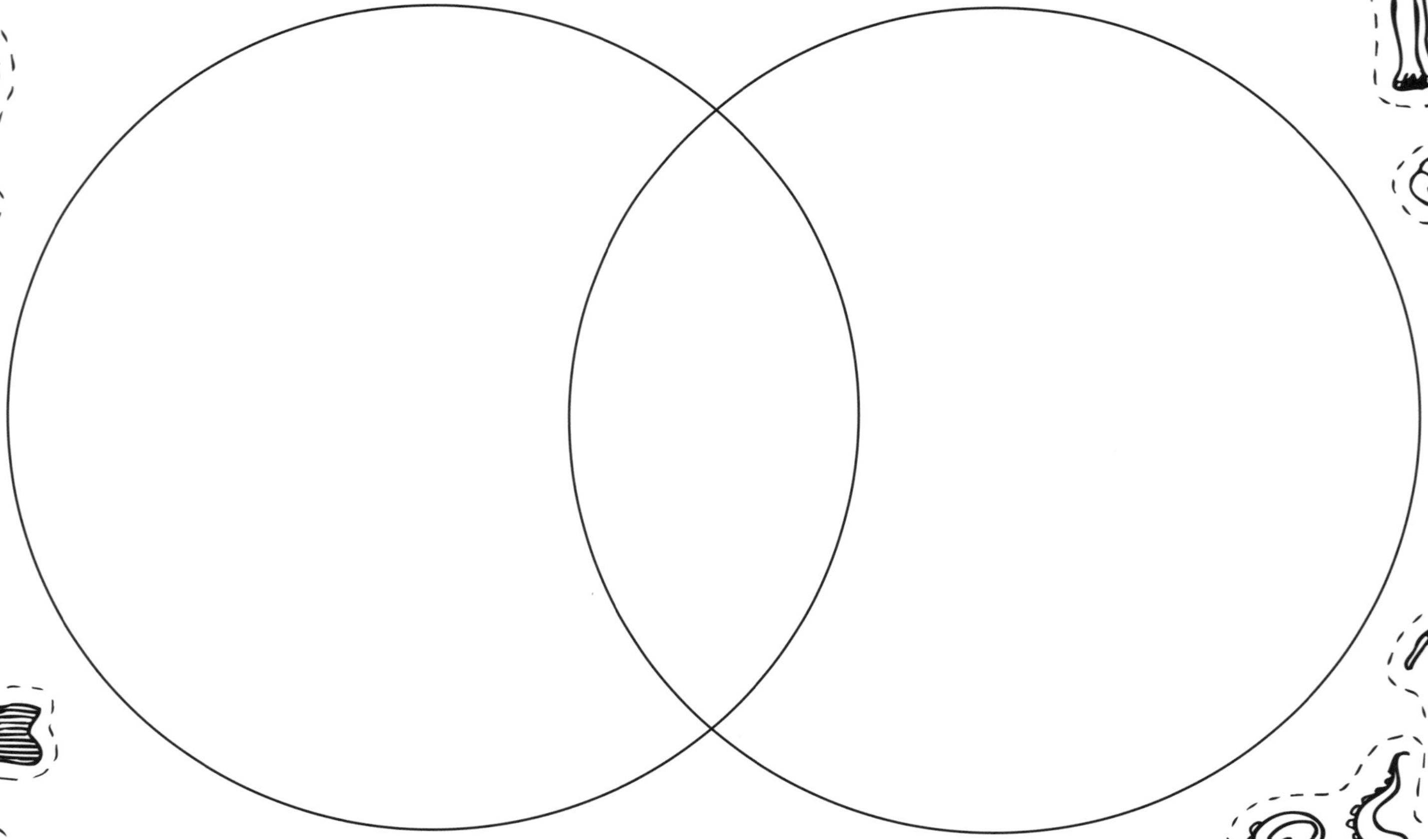

These live in **the sea**.

These live **on the land**.

SCHOLASTIC www.scholastic.co.uk

Name ______________________

Favourite colours

Ask your friends to choose a favourite colour. Colour in a square.

red									
blue									
yellow									
green									
orange									
pink									

Name ______________________________

Push, pull or twist

- How do you operate these? The first one has been done for you.

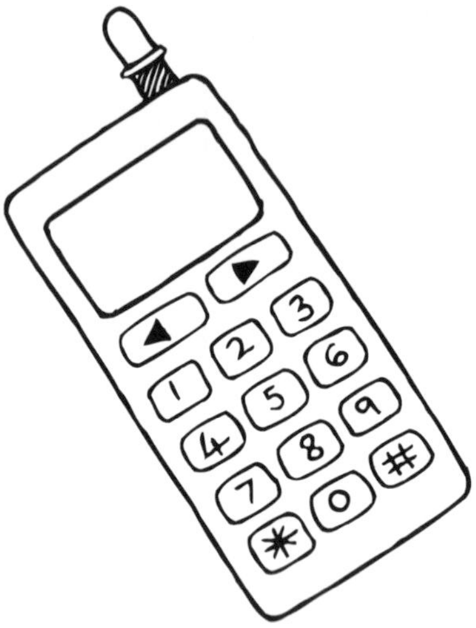

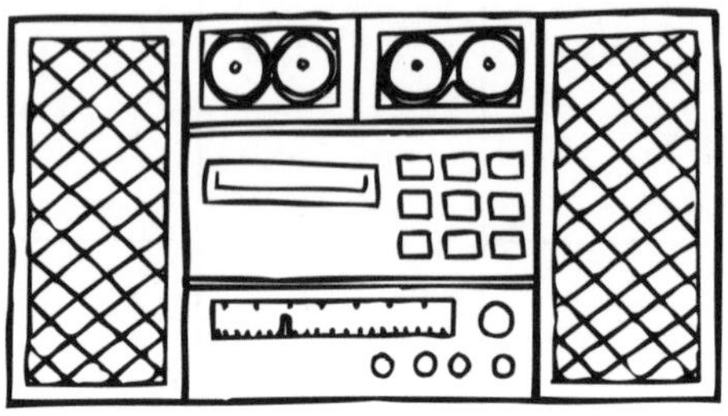

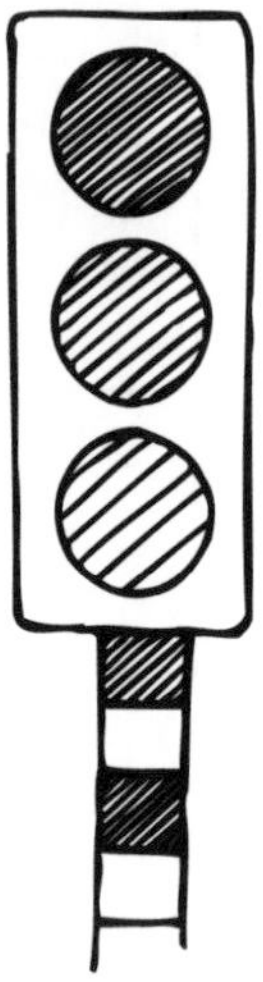

buttons

dials

switches

remote control

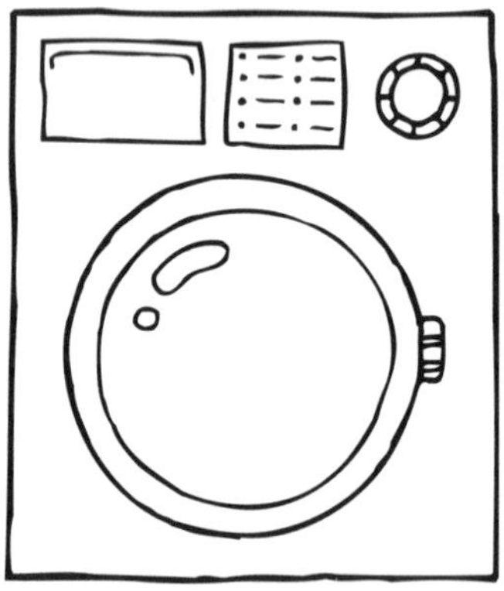

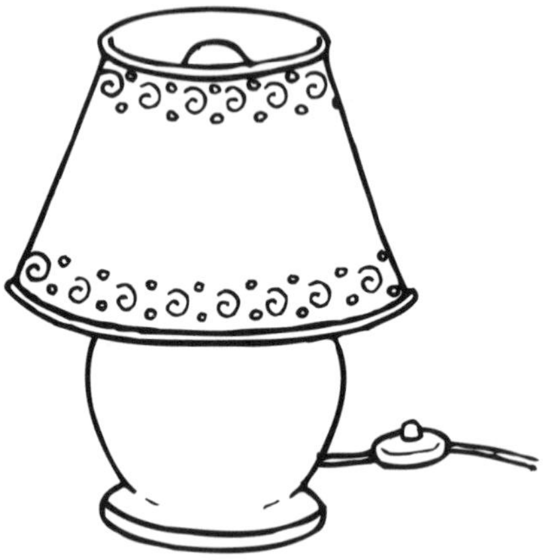

- Draw a device of your own. How do you operate it?

Name ______________________

A portrait (1)

Clemens August as Falconer by Pieter Horemans

- What is this man doing?
- What sort of person do you think he is?
- Can you describe what he is wearing?
- Why do you think he had his picture painted?
- Can you pose like this?

This man is...

Name ____________________

A portrait (2)

School Boy by Albert Anker (1875)

- Look at this boy's face.
- How old do you think he is? How can you tell?
- What is he doing?
- Can you describe what he is wearing?
- Can you pose like this?

This boy is...

SCHOLASTIC
www.scholastic.co.uk

Name ______________________

In the mirror

● Look at yourself in the mirror. Describe what you see.

I am ______________________

____

I have ______________________

____

I look like ______________________

____

● Draw your own self-portrait here.

Name ______________________________

Spot the fabric

Draw lines to show what these objects are made from.

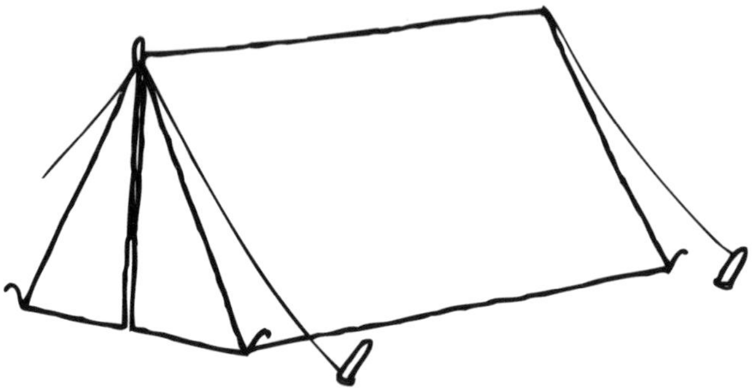

fabric

something else

Name ______________________________

Sculpture

- What is it?
- Who made it? Why?
- What do you think it is made of?
- Where would you put it?

- Make a sculpture of your own like this.

Little Red Riding Hood

- Tell the story. Use different voices for each character.

- Which voices did you use?

talking | loud | soft | whispering | rough | gentle | high | low

Name ______________________________

Making sounds

Make the sounds in this picture. What will you use to make the sounds?

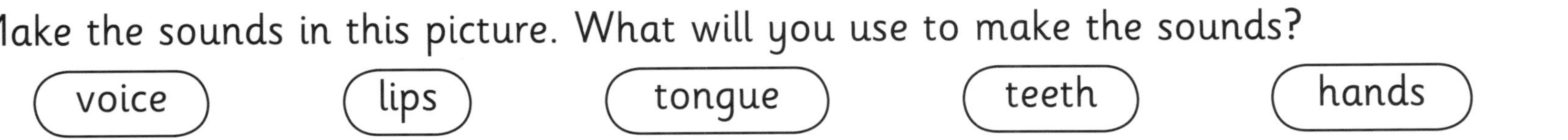

Name ______________________________

Long and short sounds

Which sound is **long** and which is **short**? The first one has been done for you.

ticking and chiming

hammering and sawing

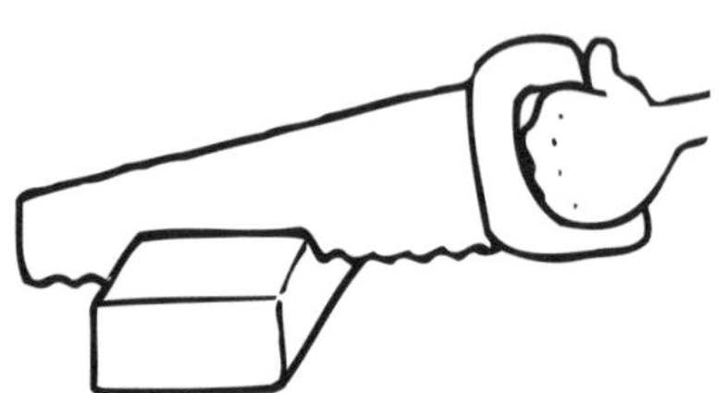

short

knocking and ringing

short

dripping and running

short

barking and growling

long

short

Name ______________________

Higher and lower

Match the dots to the songs.

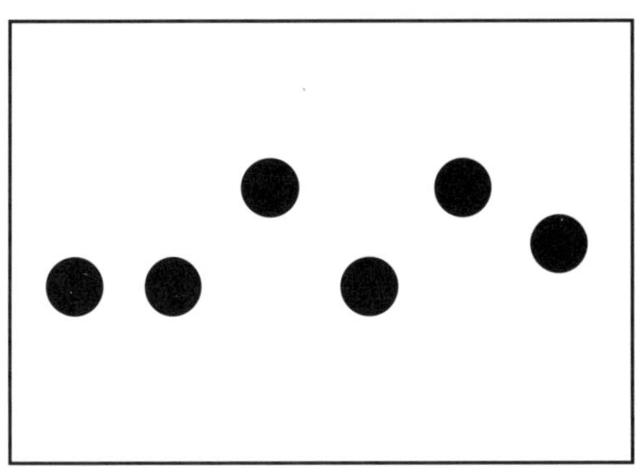

Three Blind Mice

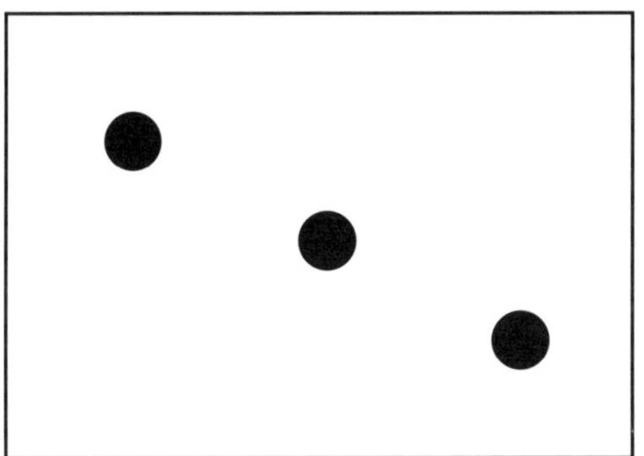

London's Burning

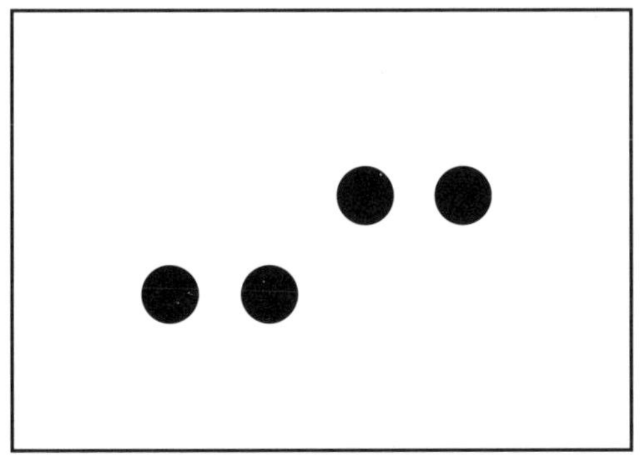

Twinkle, Twinkle Little Star

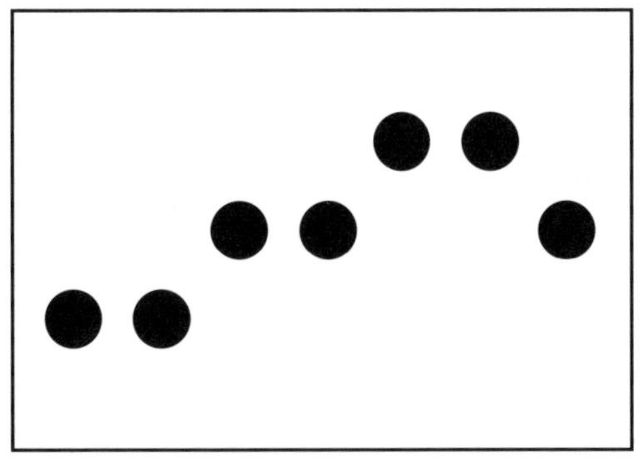

Happy Birthday to You

Name ____________________

Belonging

Which groups do you belong to? Draw them. Name them.

I belong to

the ______________ family.

I belong to

____

I belong to

____

I belong to

____

Beavers Brownies school class friends

Name ______________________________

Belonging: religion (1)

Which pictures belong to which religion?

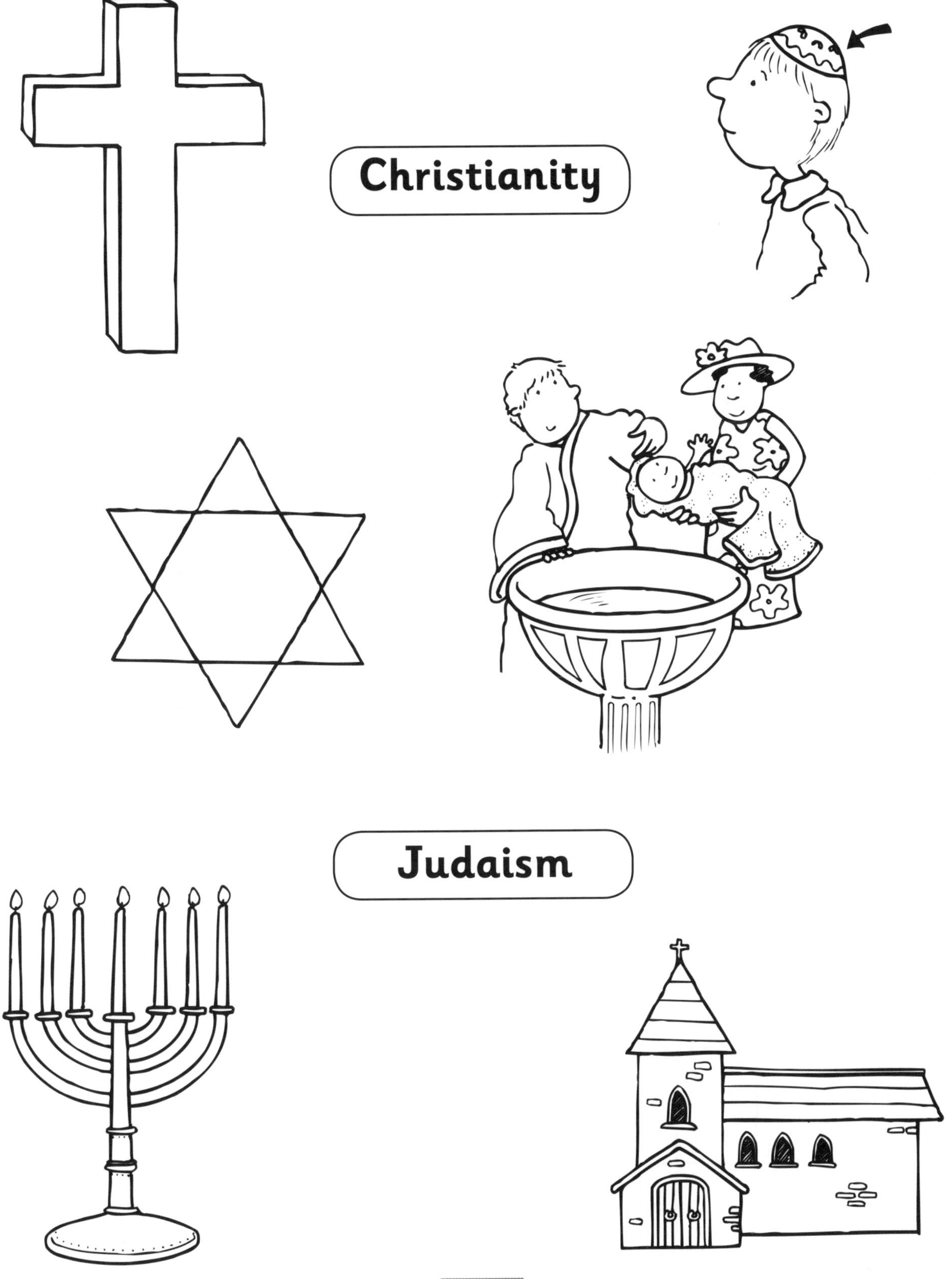

Name ____________________

Belonging: religion (2)

Which pictures belong to which religion?

SCHOLASTIC
www.scholastic.co.uk

Name ____________________

Belonging: religion (3)

Which pictures belong to which religion?

Name ______________________

Christmas gifts

Name ______________________

Belonging: Christianity

- Match these labels to the pictures.

baptism candle | cross | fish badge | font

- Complete this sentence.

I wear ______________________ because

I belong to ______________________.

Name ______________________

Welcome to our school

- Our school is a welcoming school because ______________________

____

Things to think about

signs and notices
the school entrance
smiling people
seats and furniture
pictures
books

- Draw your school entrance.

SCHOLASTIC
www.scholastic.co.uk

Name ______________________________

Good things about my friend

- My friend is called

  ____

- Draw their picture here.

- Three good things about my friend are:

1. ______________________________

____

2. ______________________________

____

3. ______________________________

____

Name ______________________

Keeping safe in school

- What is dangerous about these pictures?

Don't! Why?

Don't! Why?

Don't! Why?

- Draw your own danger.

Don't! Why?

run out of school | throw stones | play with doors

Name ______________________________

Moving house

How does this family feel about moving house?

Zak is ________________________ because he will have a room of his own.

Dad is ________________________ because the new house will not need painting.

Alice is ________________________ because she liked her old bedroom.

Mum is ________________________ because she might not get on with the new neighbours.

Kip is ________________________ because he doesn't know what is happening.

Baby is sleeping because she is

______________________.

sad | excited | pleased | tired | confused | worried

Name ____________________

Permission

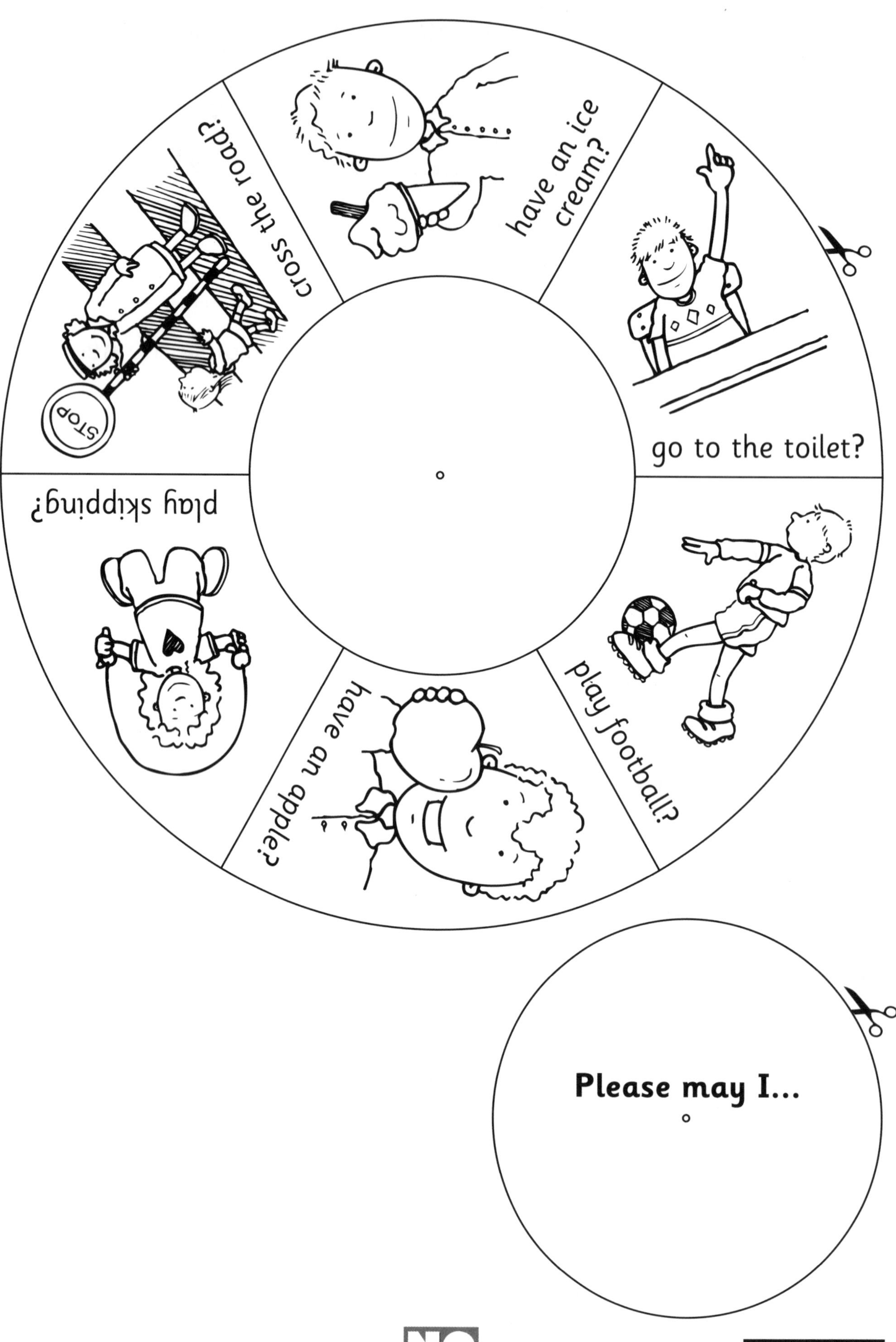

NO FUSS PHOTOCOPIABLE

Name ________________________________

I am good at...

- Choose three stamps. Cut them out and stick them in the empty boxes.

I am good at  ________________________.

I am good at  ________________________.

I am good at  ________________________.

- Draw your own picture here.

I am good at ____

football	writing	PE	reading
2+2=4			
maths	tidying up	singing	making friends

Name ______________________

Mistakes

Is it all right to...

drop a cup? Yes 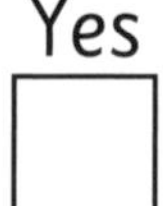 No

tread on a cat? Yes 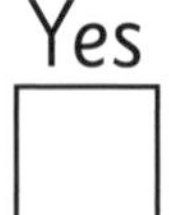 No

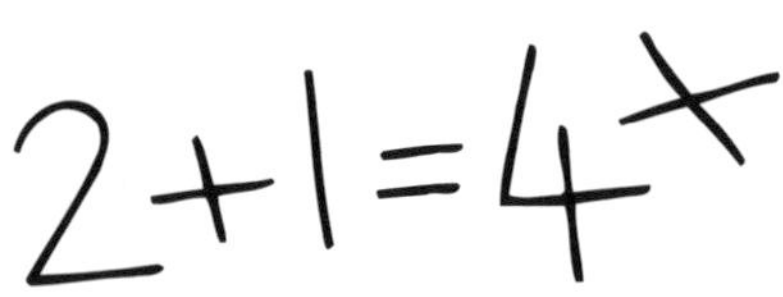

get a sum wrong? Yes 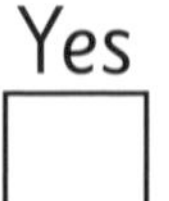 No

take the wrong hat? Yes  No

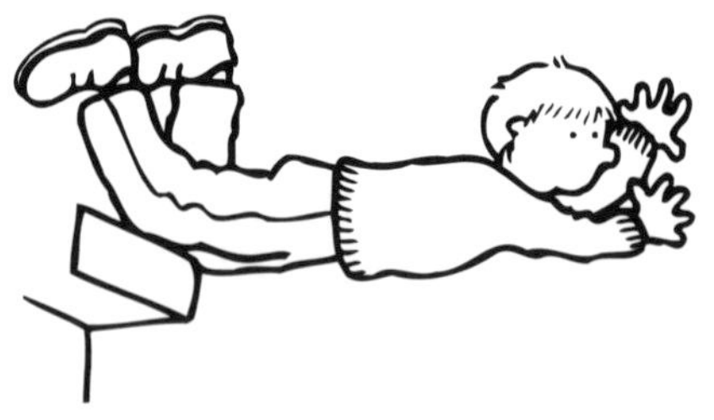

trip over the step? Yes  No

bump into the teacher? Yes  No

Name ______________________

Feelings

How is Fred feeling?

Fred is feeling...

angry	guilty	tired
thoughtful	happy	sad

SCHOLASTIC

In this series:

ISBN 978-1407-10093-7

ISBN 978-1407-10094-4

ISBN 978-1407-10095-1

ISBN 978-1407-10096-8

ISBN 978-1407-10097-5

ISBN 978-1407-10098-2

ISBN 978-0439-96548-4

ISBN 978-0439-96550-7

ISBN 978-0439-96552-1

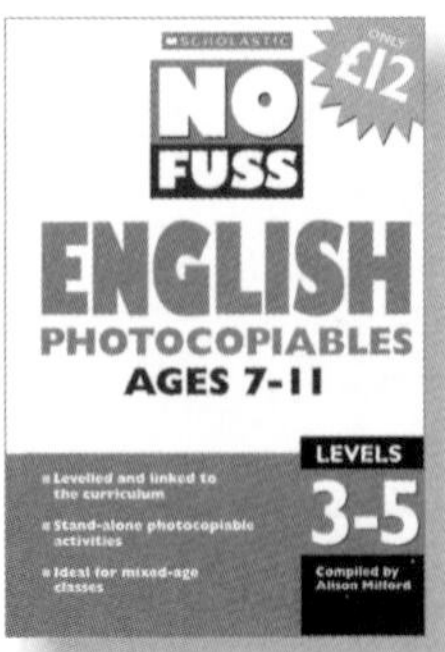

ISBN 978-0439-96549-1

ISBN 978-0439-96551-4

ISBN 978-0439-96553-8

To find out more, call: 0845 603 9091
or visit our website www.scholastic.co.uk